TAMING THE WILD OUTDOORS

Building Cooperative Learning Through Outdoor Education

Written and photographed by Mark Levin
Illustrated by Jeanette Courtin

Imprint Manager: Kristin Eclov
Senior Editors: Kathy Zahn & Christine Hood
Inside Design: Riley Wilkinson
Cover Design: Riley Wilkinson & Jonathan Wu
Digital Pre-Press: Danielle Dela Cruz
Cover Photography: Anthony Nex

GOOD APPLE
A Division of Frank Schaffer Publications
23740 Hawthorne Boulevard
Torrance, CA 90505

Table of Contents

Introduction

Why Teach Outdoor Education?

There are many reasons to teach outdoor education. For starters, kids love being outdoors! They are always ready to explore, create, and learn. Being outdoors lends excitement to lessons started in the classroom and conjures up all kinds of ways to teach a concept, hone a skill, or make a discovery. Outdoor education heightens awareness, awakens enthusiasm, and instills appreciation for the environment and the natural world.

Learning about nature and the environment is often best done outdoors. When students study the environment, insects, adaptation, or predator-prey relationships, they can only glean so much from a book. Only when students become "one with nature" do they really understand. They understand by appreciating, experiencing, and becoming acclimated to the natural world around them.

Finally, outdoor education programs are the perfect means for integrating the curriculum. Outdoor education is not just science—it is and can be every subject. A resourceful teacher will find many practical ways to cover all the disciplines in an outdoor setting. You'll find plenty of ways to combine science, math, writing, art, physical education, social studies, and more, into an outdoor education experience.

There are two "camps" in the environmental education world. One group believes in the "gather round while I tell you everything I know" approach. These leaders know their stuff and insist on telling students the name of every living and non-living thing they come across. Nothing wrong here, but kids can't remember all of this—and generally, they don't care. I have friends (those who love naming things) who will question the academic validity of such activities if students haven't learned the proper scientific names to over a dozen things while on an hour-long outing. I try to explain my philosophy—that of the other camp—which believes more in the "share and do" approach. My first goal is to get students excited about nature. I want them to see things up close, observe from a different perspective, use all their senses, imagine, and be creative. We can even make up names for objects we come across. Then, when children are ready for and really want to know the information, we can look up names in a field guide. Students will remember a great deal more when they have a desire to know something on their own terms. Both philosophies have a place in outdoor education, and both can be combined and fine tuned to the teacher's likes and abilities. Teach in the way you feel most comfortable, and enjoy!

About the Book

There are two key groups of activities in *Taming the Wild Outdoors*. The first group involves teaching about the environment and nature. Then, when you're ready, there's information on how to combine these activities into a full-day or multiple-day program. The other group of activities, group dynamics, shows you how to lead student groups into problem-solving situations and help them learn to work together as a team. These activities can be done as an entirely separate program, or combined with the environmental activities to assemble one amazing experience kids will remember long after school is over!

This resource will excite students about being outdoors as well as enhance their knowledge about nature, teaching them greater respect for their environment. Most of the activities are easy to implement and involve minimal preparation. Props and/or materials needed for each activity are listed in the activity description. Most materials are easy to find and generally "on hand" at school.

Bringing students into the "outdoor classroom" is sure to stimulate their interest in nature, as well as their knowledge of themselves and their classmates. They may even discover strengths and talents they never knew they had. Use these experiences as stepping stones to a world of adventure for your students!

One frog in the pond is worth five in formaldehyde.

—author unknown

Chapter One

Environmental Awareness/ Nature Activities

This chapter will get you and your students outdoors and into nature within minutes. Twenty hikes launch Chapter One—hikes you can take right outside your classroom door. And, like most of the activities in this book, these hikes take virtually no preparation. Your students will enjoy and appreciate the environment more and more as they participate in these activities.

The *Sensory Awareness* section contains a selection of nature activities to excite your students about the outdoors. These activities help "fine tune" your students' senses, helping them to better observe their surroundings. These are followed by additional activities designed to teach environmental concepts like the "web of life," which dramatically demonstrates how everything in nature is connected and interwoven.

In the last section, you'll find several scavenger hunts, always a student favorite. There is a ready-to-use *Scavenger Hunt List* on page 29. Note that none of these scavenger hunts involve collecting actual items. Students are instructed to find items, check them off, and leave them exactly where they were found.

Chapter One concludes with several more simple activities, including things to do after dark, as well as activities that can be ongoing throughout the school year, such as *Magic Spots* and *Adopt-a-Tree*. You will find ready-to-use activity sheets at the end of the chapter.

Note: As with any field trip, you will need to take certain precautions and follow certain school procedures. This is true for any and all activities in this book, even if you're only going right outside your classroom. For example, you may want to know who is allergic to bee stings. Most of these activities can be easily handled by the classroom teacher, though any time you can enlist the help of a parent volunteer, do so. This helps with "crowd control," enabling you to break the class down into smaller groups, if you wish.

Hikes at School

Nothing stimulates excitement more than hearing the words, *We're going on a hike today.* Hikes can take place anywhere, including right outside your classroom! The following hikes are easy to lead, fun to take, and can extend to a myriad of activities back in the classroom.

Blind Hike

There are several ways to lead this special experience. If your students are older and can be trusted to genuinely help and take care of each other, you could blindfold half of them while the other half leads as "sighted" students. The sighted students gently lead blindfolded students around as they help them tune in to their senses. They can sniff things, touch things, and listen

carefully to their surroundings. After several minutes, have students switch places.

As a variation, run a long piece (50–100 feet; 30–50 meters) of rope or nylon cord along a prearranged route. All students are blindfolded and led to the starting point. Each student places his or her hand on the rope as a guide and slowly walks (or crawls) the route. Tell students to take time to smell, listen, and feel as they walk. Start students at intervals of either several feet (meters) or a minute's time. When they get to the end of the rope, have them record their discoveries and thoughts in their journals.

100 Inches (250 Centimeters) Hike

This is a hike to the "micro-world." Begin by telling students that they are going on a hike. Explain that while most people go on hikes many miles long, this one will be only 100 inches (250 cm). Tell students they are going to get close to nature and see things most others pass by.

For this hike, each student needs 100 inches (250 cm) of string, a hand lens, and five to eight craft sticks. Have students get on their hands and knees and place their string along the ground like a hiking trail. It can go over old tree stumps, around a tree trunk, over a rock, and so on. Each time students find something they want to share, they stick a "sign post" (craft stick) next to it. Invite students to "name" their trails based on a natural phenomenon, such as "Old Man's Wart Trail" for a trail featuring an old tree stump. Encourage students to observe only when on their hands and knees, and to look at objects through their hand lenses.

After they've finished discovering and designing their trails, divide the group into pairs, and let each student take turns leading tours. Finish this activity with a sharing circle and invite each student to share his or her favorite "find" on the trail.

A variation on the *100 Inches Hike* is *Micro Park*. For this activity, a student uses the string to encircle his or her special park. He or she likewise uses the craft sticks to mark unusual and interesting natural features. The student can then lead tours for an admiring public.

ABC Hike

This no-preparation hike tests students' creativity and powers of observation. Using pages 27 and 28 or a blank piece of paper, tell students, either individually or in small groups, to look for natural objects whose names start with each letter of the alphabet. Younger students can draw their alphabet finds directly on the pages, while older students can write what they see in the space next to each letter. Have them start with "A," and explain that they can't go onto "B" and subsequent letters until they've found something that begins with "A." A good rule is to require that the items students find are "natural" as opposed to person-made. You can decide for your class if that will be a rule. Often, you'll have to allow such creative discoveries as crossed twigs for the letter "X." Children will find that some letters are much harder to discover than others. End the hike with a sharing circle.

Heads and Tails Hike

This hike is an excellent excitement builder. Explain to students that you have not determined a specific route for the hike. You or a student can flip a coin. If it comes up heads, you turn right. If it comes up tails, you turn left. Continue to walk and explore until you come to an unhikeable obstacle, then flip the coin again. Students love the "sense of the unknown," even if it's in their own backyards.

Animal Homes Hike

Have students look for animal homes in all kinds of habitats. A tree is a good place to start. Tell students that animals live in different parts of the tree—canopy, branches, under bark, and under roots. Students should also look under fallen logs. Caution them to be careful when turning over a log, and to replace the log exactly as it was found. Students can also look in tall grass, bushes, standing water, cracks in sidewalks, and under eaves of buildings. Invite them to draw pictures of the various animal homes they find.

Freaks of Nature Hike

The emphasis of this hike is to look for "natural oddities." You might find a huge oak tree gall, a tree trunk with new shoots growing out of it, the "world's largest fungus," and so on. Kids love to invent superlatives to go along with their discoveries.

Silent Hike

The emphasis of this hike is on the sense of hearing. No talking is allowed. Have students write questions, make notes, or draw things they observe. Also, have them keep track of the natural sounds they hear.

Tree Hike

On this hike, students look for a variety of tree-related superlatives such as *tallest, smallest, greenest, most leafy, roughest bark,* and so on. You can even have students classify trees into categories such as *evergreen* or *deciduous.*

Bird Hike

Tell students to make a list of all the birds they see on this hike. Have them note the birds' physical characteristics so they can look them up in a field guide later.

Tracking Hike

Send one student (or group) out early to mark a trail using markers (e.g., small squares of colored construction paper or "camouflaged" insects made from pipe cleaners). The rest of the class then goes on the hike looking for these hidden markers.

Human Camera Hike

This is a wonderful activity for partners. One student becomes the human camera, and the other, the photographer. The "photographer" puts his or her hands on the shoulders of the "camera" and guides him or her (whose eyes are tightly shut) carefully around to face various wonderful scenes. When the camera is correctly positioned, the photographer gently squeezes his or her shoulders. This opens the "shutter," allowing the camera to see the scene. The camera only opens his or her eyes for a second. The photographer then walks the camera over to the next scene and repeats. Photographers can choose a variety of "lenses"—close-up, telephoto, wide angle, and so on, depending on the desired view. After a few minutes, have students switch roles. When both students have had a chance to be the camera, invite them to discuss their favorite scenes, or "photos."

Shapes and Patterns Hike

Invite students to look for shapes, patterns, and textures in nature. Have them sketch these in their journals.

Rainbow Hike

On this hike, emphasize colors and variations of those colors.

Follow an Ant Hike

Tell students to attempt to follow one ant (or similar creature) for a few minutes. Have them observe this creature's habits and record them in their journals.

Sound Experience Hike

Take a hike around your school grounds or in the woods. Stop every three to five minutes and tell students to be absolutely still. Then have them sit down and close their eyes and listen for one minute. Students should make mental notes of every sound they hear. Then invite them to report the different sounds they heard. Were the sounds natural, person-made, constant, fleeting? Continue on your hike to a new stopping point and start over.

Quality of Nature Hike

Take a hike around your school campus/town/park to observe the quality of nature there. Have students record their findings in their journals. Students can check for litter, graffiti, vandalism, trampled vegetation, eroded trails, sick trees, unpleasant odors, and signs of pollution. Let students rate the area on a scale of one to ten, and use this as a comparison to other areas you visit.

"I'm Not Moving Until I See Some Wildlife" Hike

On this hike, students find a place to sit and remain very still and quiet until they have individually spotted some wildlife. This doesn't have to be something big, like a fox. It can be something much smaller and just as important, such as an ant, bee, bird, squirrel, or spider.

"I'm Not Moving Until I've Written a Poem" Hike

Let students' creativity with nature flow. Take them out and encourage them to write and illustrate rhyming, free-verse, haiku, cinquain, or other poems. Encourage students to share their poems with others.

"We're Not Moving Until We've Written a Poem" Hike

A variation on the previous activity is to write a group poem. Place students in different sensory positions to observe a single tree. Invite them to describe the tree from their points of view by providing two adjectives. Some students might be placed with their heads tilted toward the tree's canopy; others might focus on the root system; others might have a close-up view of the bark; and others might focus on just one branch. Several other students may be blindfolded and asked to describe the tree using their sense of touch or smell. Finally, others may have a "wide-angle" view of the entire tree. Ask a volunteer to record the adjectives from each student. Collectively, students then create a class poem. Give a dramatic reading of this poem as everyone gets another chance to see the whole tree.

Owl Prowls

Any hike you take at night will be memorable. If it is a moonlit night, try at least part of the hike without using flashlights. You could also tape red cellophane over flashlights and let students look for nocturnal creatures.

Nature Activities: Sensory Awareness

Everyone loves games. The activities in this section teach environmental concepts, stimulate the senses, and peak your students' curiosity.

Last Detail

This wonderful activity is the perfect way to start the process of helping students learn to observe with keen eyes. Divide your class into two groups and have them line up facing each other. There should be about four feet (1 meter) of space between the two lines. Have students sit down in their two lines, facing each other. Each student should have a partner opposite him or her. Tell students that in a minute, they are going to observe "every little detail" about their partners, including what they're wearing, how they're wearing it, how jewelry is arranged, how shoes are tied, how hair is combed, and so on. Let students observe for one or two minutes. Say *stop,* and have students turn their backs to each other. Then ask them to make changes in their appearance by changing the way their clothes, hair, jewelry, and so on, is arranged. Give them three or four minutes to make these changes.

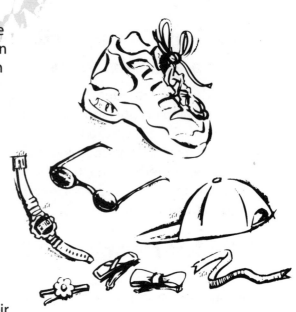

Students usually get really creative at this point, but some may need a few suggestions. For instance, students could take off socks, switch shoes to the other feet, pull up sleeves, undo hair, take off glasses, push socks down around ankles, unbutton buttons, button buttons, exchange some items with another student, and even turn shirts backward. There will be plenty of chuckles as students go through their transformations.

After everyone has had a chance to change their appearance, tell students to turn back around so they're facing each other again. Next, have students take turns seeing how many of the changes they can discover.

Conclude this activity by asking who had the most changes, who found all the changes, who had the most creative changes, and so on.

Sleeping Miser

This game is wonderful for teaching kids to listen and use their sense of hearing. *Sleeping Miser* can get a whole group of rowdy youngsters to settle down in a hurry! Choose one student to be the miser. Blindfold this student and have him or her sit down with a rolled-up bandanna or a natural object (pinecone) placed in front of him or her. Next, choose one student to be the leader. The remaining students are stalkers. Have "stalkers" form a circle around the "miser," at least ten feet (three meters) away. The leader points to a stalker, who then attempts to creep in quietly and "sneak" the object away from the miser. The miser concentrates on locating the sound of the stalker. When the miser hears movement, he or she points to the sound. The leader makes a quick judgment call, saying *yes* or *no*. Any hesitation on the leader's part may help the miser realize just how close he or she might be to stopping the stalker.

Give the miser three chances to make a "hit," which stops the stalker in his or her tracks. If the miser successfully stops a stalker, the stalker remains in the middle, and the leader points to another stalker who will now attempt to grab the treasure. If a stalker successfully gets to the miser and grabs the treasure, he or she then becomes the miser.

Sleeping Miser can lead to good follow-up discussion after play is completed. Questions to ponder include: *Does ground cover make a difference in an animal's ability to stalk its prey? Does it make a difference which way the wind is blowing? Does being blind increase the sense of hearing?*

Sound Symphony

This simple activity will amaze students as they hear all kinds of sounds that they usually take for granted. Have students choose a place to sit outside and close their eyes. They should not make any sounds for 60 seconds. (Many will claim that it seems like an hour, and others will want to continue.) While listening, have them mentally count and remember all the sounds they hear. After the minute is up, discuss the sounds students heard. Ask them to distinguish between "natural" and "human-made" sounds.

Envirolopes

This activity (from the OBIS series—see Resources, page 122) keeps students active while presenting them with several sensory challenges in a rapid-fire activity. Prepare a set of heavy-duty manila envelopes by writing a challenge relating to the environment and the outdoors on each one. Challenges can include finding five examples of different shades of green, five examples of different shades of brown, five different seeds, five different rocks, five different textures, five different odors, five signs of animal life, five fuzzy objects, and so on.

Find Five Signs of Animal Life.
1. bird nest
2. deer tracks
3. rabbit burrow
4. empty acorn shells
5. bird feathers

Make sure you have enough envelopes for each group of two or three students. Give students their "envirolopes" and explain that everything they find should be able to be returned to the place of discovery without any harm being done. As students bring in their filled envirolopes, trade one challenge for another, and send them back out. Close by having everyone form a sharing circle and relate one neat discovery.

Images

Have students sit in a circle either inside or outside. Choose one leader in each group. If you have a large group, divide them into smaller groups of six to seven. Find one natural object in the area for each group, such as a large lichen-covered branch, pinecone, piece of bark, handful of topsoil, fist-sized rock, and so on. Tell the groups that you're going to start moving an object around the circle, and each person will take a turn describing it. Students will have to use all of their senses (except taste) to describe the object. There are two rules students must follow: First, a student should not stop describing the object until the leader says *pass;* and second, a student cannot say something that someone else has already mentioned. This means group members will need to really tune in to what others are saying.

You can speed up or slow down the "pass" command according to how the game is going. You can also swap the objects between various groups, even before everyone has had a chance to talk. This activity increases students' creativity as they "dig deep" to find new ways of describing familiar things.

Nature Duplication

Before this activity begins, collect 20 natural objects from around the study area. Bring the objects to the activity site; place them on a tray, a bench, or the ground; and cover them with a towel. Tell students they have 60 seconds to stare at the objects and memorize what they see. After time is up, cover the objects. Tell students (in teams of two or three) to make lists of everything on the tray. Give groups five minutes to complete their lists. Then reassemble all students and unveil the objects. Hold up each object and tell students to check it off on their lists if they've written it down.

A variation of this game is for groups to go out and attempt to find matching objects in the study area to duplicate the objects that were uncovered. Remember, every item should be returned safely to its original location when the game is over.

Meet a Tree

This favorite activity enables students to become well acquainted with a special tree using their senses of touch and smell. Take students to a forested area, though any area with a few trees will do. Divide the group into pairs and blindfold one student in each pair. Each blindfolded student is then twirled around a few times by his or her partner and walked over to a particular tree. You can make this a little more intriguing and difficult by having partners walk the blindfolded students in and around the area before settling on each student's special tree. Each blindfolded student then gets to "meet" his or her tree. He or she uses the senses of touch and smell to get to know the tree. The student should "examine" the tree for size, special textural characteristics, locations of low branches, unusual root formations, and so on. After the blindfolded student has had enough time to be properly "introduced" to the tree, a sighted student should again walk him or her randomly around the area and back to the starting point. Remove the blindfold and encourage that student to try and find his or her tree. Afterwards, have partners switch roles. Good discussion can follow about what helped blindfolded students find their trees.

Team Sense

In this activity, groups of four blindfolded students work together to experience and describe an object. One person can smell, another can taste (be cautious here), another can hear, and the last can touch. Each team member describes the object to other team members using only one sense. Then, invite groups to attempt to identify their objects.

Nature Activities: Concept Building

Web of Life

This activity is a perennial favorite in just about any environmental awareness program, and for good reason. *Web of Life* does a wonderful job of teaching the concept that everything in nature is connected to everything else. For this activity, you will need a ball of twine, string, or yarn; 5" x 8" (12.5 cm x 20 cm) note cards or sheets of paper; and a marker.

There are several ways to set up this activity. You can predetermine what lives in the area or ecosystem you're studying and write the names of everything (plants, animals, water sources, sun) on the cards or paper. The other option is to have students call out what lives in the area while you jot the names down on the cards. Students will often go overboard when thinking of what lives in the area and will come up with some species that are probably two continents away. Include only those that are known inhabitants of your locale.

Attempt to have enough components of the ecosystem so that every student has a card. Have students stand in a large circle while you start the process of connecting each component to the other components according to which ones depend on others for life. Use the string or yarn for connecting. For example, a squirrel might have a string attached from it to a tree and to a water source; the tree might be attached to the sun, the water source, and the soil; a bird might be connected to the tree, the water source, and even to an insect or earthworm. Eventually, everything is connected, cross connected, and connected again with just about everything in the circle. (Make sure students hold the string tightly.)

After all connections have been made, the real discussion begins. Students will quickly see how everything in life seems to be connected with just about everything else. Discuss what happens when just one component is missing (maybe it became extinct or moved on because of a dwindling food supply). Have a student holding a particular set of strings give a slight tug to demonstrate that just about every string moves. Repeat this with other components and help students understand the interrelationships among living things. Invite students to verbalize their discoveries.

Bats and Moths

This activity is an excellent way to teach students about the echolocation abilities of a bat searching out its prey. Bats love moths and other insects, but they need a lot of them to get full. So a successful bat in this game is going to need to be quick!

Choose one student to be a bat and one to be a moth. The rest of the students make a large circle around the two and serve as the boundaries or environmental range of this particular "bat." The bat is blindfolded. Explain that bats aren't really blind, but depend on their keen hearing to locate prey. To begin, the bat runs around the inner circle looking for its prey—the "moth." In order for the bat to eat and survive, it must tag the moth. This isn't very easy for a blindfolded bat, so the bat needs to depend on its sense of echolocation. The bat calls out the word *bat* to locate the moth. The moth serves as a bounce-back object and says *moth*. Each time the bat says *bat,* the moth should instantly respond with *moth*. The bat quickly learns to continually say *bat, bat, bat . . .* in order to find the moth.

For a variation, try putting in a couple of moths, or closing up or increasing the diameter of the circle. Stand by to make sure the bat stays safely within the play zone.

Discussion can follow the game about what helped the blindfolded bat find its "dinner." The answer is *echolocation*—a sensory system in certain animals in which high-pitched sounds are emitted and their echoes interpreted to determine the direction and distance of objects.

The Four Secrets of Life

For this guessing activity, place a small jar of soil, a small vial of water, and a picture of the sun inside a small box. Note that air gets in naturally. These are "the four secrets of life." If you want to include "shelter" as another secret of life, add a picture of a house or nest.

Place the box inside a bag, and then inside another bag, and again inside another. This will really pique students' interest when you tell them that the four secrets of life are inside the bags. Have students start guessing, and then write everything they say on the board. Don't comment on any of their choices.

Once you finish making the list, ceremoniously begin taking the bags out of the bags until you get to the box. Then, dramatically open the lid of the box. At that point, have students look at the list and circle those four (or five) "secrets of life"!

Food-Chain Game

This game from OBIS *(Outdoor Biology Instructional Strategies)* provides a fun, fast-moving outdoor game designed to teach about food chains and the balance of nature. The goal for each player is to survive as an "animal" by getting enough to eat while avoiding being eaten.

To play this game, you will need 4–5 liters of popcorn, chart paper, marking pens, plastic sandwich bags, masking tape, and 5-inch (12.5-cm) square construction-paper cards in red and green. Have enough of each color for about two-thirds of your students. The sandwich bags will become "stomach bags." Place a strip of masking tape across each sandwich bag so that the bottom edge of the tape is 1/2 inch (1.25 cm) from the bottom.

Choose a site approximately 50 feet (15 m) square. (You can change this to make the game easier or more challenging.) Ask students if they know what eats mice and what mice eat. They may respond with *Mice eat seeds, and snakes eat mice.* Then ask them what might eat snakes. For the benefit of this game, use the answer *hawks.* Diagram the relationship students describe, and introduce it as a food chain. Ask students if they can think of other food chains, including one with humans.

How to Play

1. Describe the play area boundaries. Then spread popcorn over the area. Tell students you are distributing the plants that grasshoppers eat.

2. Give plastic bags to one-third of your students. These students will be grasshoppers. When you say *go,* "grasshoppers" place "food" (popcorn) in their "stomachs" (bags).

3. Give bags and green cards to a second one-third of the group, and red cards to the last third. When the game starts, "frogs" (green cards) try to capture (tag) grasshoppers, and "hawks" (red cards) pursue frogs. When a frog captures a grasshopper, the grasshopper's stomach is transferred to the frog. When a hawk captures a frog, he or she takes the frog's stomach. Hawks do not eat grasshoppers in this game. Frogs and hawks must visibly carry their green and red cards, or you can attach them to students' clothing with clothespins or tape.

4. The first game usually lasts only a few seconds with one of two things happening: Grasshoppers are gobbled up before they have a chance to forage, or frogs are gobbled up, and grasshoppers continue to eat popcorn and get fat.

Following the game, lead a discussion with students. How many of each kind of animal survived? For a grasshopper to survive, popcorn must fill the stomach bag to the bottom of the tape. For a frog to survive, popcorn must fill the stomach bag to the top of the tape. Hawks must have the equivalent of one frog with sufficient food to survive. If at least one of each kind of animal survives, you have an ongoing food chain. Return the popcorn to the activity area after each game. Each round of play equals a day in the life of this food chain.

Ask students to suggest rule variations that may result in more of a balance after each playing cycle, or a day in the life of these creatures. Usually one rule is changed for each replay so students can see if it works. Students can use chart paper to record rule changes and population changes before and after each round. Tell them to remember that they are trying to end each day with at least one of each animal alive and kicking. After each game, analyze the results. How many grasshoppers got a full stomach? How many frogs? hawks?

With enough playing time and enough times at trying new starting numbers for each animal, students come to realize that an area needs many, many more things at the bottom of the food chain than at the top. Generally, based on an energy chain pyramid, you would need ten frogs for each hawk, 100 grasshoppers for each frog, and 1,000 units of grasshopper food (popcorn) for each grasshopper to survive. Please note that these numbers are only broad rules of thumb.

Some variables you could add to this game include:

- Change the number of grasshoppers and/or frogs and/or hawks.

- Let each grasshopper come back as another grasshopper once after being captured and transferring "stomach" contents.

- Provide a "safety zone" for frogs and/or grasshoppers where they can be safe.

- Schedule timed releases. Let grasshoppers go first to forage unbothered. One minute later, release the frogs, and later, the hawks.

- Spread out more popcorn.

More Simple Activities

Scavenger Hunts

Kids love scavenger hunts! It's best to custom-design a scavenger hunt list for natural items generally found in your "hunt area." For your convenience, a reasonably generic *Scavenger Hunt List* can be found on page 29. Students should not actually collect the items. Instead, they check each item off as they see it. You can have a "promise to actually see the item" ceremony before beginning.

Don't worry about speed. Encourage students to find as many items as possible within a given time limit. Also, awarding prizes for coming in first is not a good idea, as students tend to check off items they haven't really seen. If you are interested in keeping score, you might assign a point value to each item on the list. Harder to find items can be worth premium points, while easy to find items can be worth one point. You can also assign "rankings" to various point totals, such as Chief Naturalist, Eagle Eye, and Scout.

Scavenger Hunt Themes

You can introduce a wide variety of themes into scavenger hunts as a means of teaching environmental concepts. Examples include:

Adaptation Scavenger Hunt—Look for natural items that show they've adapted to an area. A list might include lichen, grass growing in a sidewalk crack, or a seed that can "travel."

Rotting Log Hunt—Look for items related to life on a decomposing log.

Balance of Nature Hunt—Look for items that help other things in nature survive, such as "something that helps a turtle."

Mystery Bag

Find several natural objects and place each into a separate bag. Have a student look inside and describe the object to the rest of the group without giving obvious clues. Invite the group to guess the object's identity. The student who guesses correctly gets to give clues for the next object.

Mystery Passenger

For this guessing game, research a variety of plants and animals that live in your area. Write down eight to ten facts about each item, and then list these as clues in order of difficulty from hardest to easiest. Explain that you're going to start by giving one clue each day about something that shares Earth with us. You may want to put out a box with scrap paper and pencils for students' answers, otherwise they tend to shout out their guesses. This also allows you to read student guesses at your leisure. If there is no winner the first day, read the second clue along with the original clue the next day. Continue reading clues until someone wins. When there is a winner, read through all the clues again. Children like this activity so much that they usually volunteer to make up their own clues for nature objects of their choice using nature books and encyclopedias. For example:

1. *I am a mammal.*
2. *I live in trees.*
3. *I have large black eyes.*
4. *My coat is grayish brown above, and white below.*
5. *I have a flat gray-brown tail.*
6. *I have a "built-in" parachute, or sail, between my forelegs and hind legs.*
7. *I "glide" from tree to tree.*

Answer: Southern Flying Squirrel

Animal Charades

This guessing game helps students think about animals' various attributes. Beforehand, write the names of at least as many different animals as you have students in your class. Then tape the name of an animal to each student's back. Have students ask each other clues about their animals' identities until each knows what animal he or she "is."

Noah's Ark

This is a great nature game to promote group dynamics. Start by preparing animal cards. You will need two cards for each animal and a pair of animals for every two students. Choose animals whose sounds are easy to imitate, such as a monkey, horse, cow, duck, frog, donkey, human, dog, or cat. Throw in a few animals whose sounds are harder to mimic, such as a worm, mouse, or bat.

Divide the class into two groups and move them to opposite ends of the playing area. This game works well both indoors and out. Once the two groups are separated, give each student an animal card. Each card you distribute should match a card someone in the other group receives. (If you have an odd number of participants, more than two animals of a type can be included.) Tell students to find their animal partners using only sound. When you give the signal, students on each side of the playing area begin making the sounds of their animals in hopes of finding their partners. This is especially fun, and difficult, as each student should be blindfolded. Place "spotters" around the playing area to make sure no one walks into something dangerous, and of course, no running is allowed.

Once partners have found each other, have them double-check by repeating their sounds to each other a few times. Then, they can remove their blindfolds and watch the rest of the group. It's actually quite hilarious!

Adopt-a-Tree

This wonderful activity encourages students to use all of their senses, while helping them develop an appreciation for the variety of trees that grow in a specific area. While you will need an area with trees, you don't have to worry about having a national forest next door—even the most urban city centers work well.

Invite students to choose a special tree that will be theirs to study all year. They will return to it from time to time to observe and record the changes seasons and time bring. Use the *Adopt-a-Tree* form on page 30, or create your own based on your students' needs.

Magic Spots

A magic spot is a special place chosen by a student for the whole year. It's a place he or she can go to read, write, draw, or think. This might be the same spot chosen for the *Adopt-a-Tree* activity, or someplace entirely new. It should be a spot comfortable enough for the student to sit for 20 or 30 minutes. Students respect their magic spot by using it wisely. They should enter it in a hushed manner and should respect the "magic" of their classmates' spots as well by not shouting or otherwise disturbing these times and places. You will need to set limits on how far away or far apart magic spots should be.

Dinosaur Dig

Dinosaurs have always been a big hit with kids. So why not organize a dinosaur dig? Hosting your own dig is a great way to teach students archaeological and paleontology skills that include methodical excavating and follow-up scientific research. Start by finding posters and pictures of various dinosaurs. Cut these pictures into pieces and laminate them. Find a "burial site," generally a large sand play area. Use string and stakes to section this area into study grids. Bury your dinosaurs (puzzle pieces) in grids by "state." For example, you might label one grid *Colorado*, and another, *Montana*. Set up a research station with dinosaur books, and give each student a copy of the *Dinosaur Dig* activity sheet (page 31) for listing basic facts about identifying dinosaurs, such as where the dinosaur was found, its size, food source, and so on.

As students find each new puzzle piece, have teams begin putting their findings together, and then go to the research station to attempt to identify their discovery. Students should record facts and other interesting bits of information. At the end of the activity, teams come together to share what they've found.

For added excitement, bury a few plastic dinosaurs and clean chicken bones with the puzzle pieces. You could also bury pieces on the boundary between states, which means teams might only find half of what they need. Teams then work together to uncover the entire dinosaur.

In the Dumps

Garbage doesn't just disappear, or does it? This is a good activity for when students say, *But it's biodegradable!* or *The squirrels will eat it,* after they throw orange peels on the ground. In this activity, students learn the terms *decomposition, biodegradable, landfill,* and *compost* as you demonstrate how a landfill works.

Begin by having students collect several types of garbage from around the school. Include solid waste (pieces of wood, pencils, aluminum cans, plastic pencil boxes) as well as organic waste (lunchroom leftovers).

Set aside an area of the playground for your landfill area and mark it off with stakes and cord—properly signed as "Study Area—Do Not Disturb." Leave some of the trash on top of the ground and bury others at various depths. The trash on top might need to be secured with tent-type stakes and screen wire in order to keep those pesky squirrels from proving you wrong after all. Section off your mini-landfill in grids so you can record the date, what was buried and how deep, and what was left in each grid. Encourage students to come back and observe the landfill twice a week. After a month or so, let students dig up what was buried and see what remains. It is very likely that everything will be found pretty much as it was left. This will lead to some great discussions on where all of this trash goes. Why do some things decompose quicker than others? Are there things that never decompose?

You can follow-up this activity with a trip to a real city or county landfill. Talk about an eye-opening experience!

Sharing Circles

A sharing circle is a quiet way of bringing morning or afternoon activities to an end. It's wonderful for bringing closure to a whole program as well. Have students sit in a circle. The leader offers a topic—a statement that each student will complete with a simple answer. Below are some good *Sharing Circle* topics.

- *My favorite thing about the experience was . . .*
- *The neatest thing I saw today was . . .*
- *I got to know my classmates better when . . .*
- *One memory I don't think I'll ever forget is . . .*
- *The most exciting thing that happened was . . .*
- *The most important thing that happened today (this week) was . . .*
- *Two words that describe how I felt during this program are . . .*
- *The thing that bothered me most about this experience was . . .*
- *Today I learned that . . .*
- *Today I discovered . . .*
- *Nature is important to me because . . .*
- *I want to learn more about . . .*
- *One of the hardest things for me to do was . . .*
- *For the first time in my life, I . . .*
- *The thing that took the most courage was . . .*

The Magic Bag

Whenever I lead a hike or conduct most environmental education activities, I carry my Magic Bag with me. The Magic Bag is a day pack filled with all kinds of wonderful tools for "spicing up" any outdoor adventure. The most important role of a leader is to spark children's enthusiasm for nature. The Magic Bag enables you to become an "expert facilitator." By having a well-stocked bag, you can guide students to find answers on their own. A Magic Bag should contain:

Several Guide Books
Golden Guides are great! Include titles of things you might see, such as birds, trees, reptiles, insects, and flowers.

Plastic Bug Boxes
These small boxes with built-in magnifying lenses are available from educational supply stores and science equipment catalogs.

Bug Cages
These can also be bought, or made from recycled plastic containers with lids.

Binoculars

Audubon Bird Calls
These excite kids about birds, even if the call doesn't bring any in for closer observation. (You can also make a "pishhh, pishhh" sound, which imitates a bird in distress. Often birds will fly closer to see what all the fuss is about. However, only one person should do this, because if birds hear a whole class "pishhhing," they will go in the opposite direction!)

Blindfolds
Bandannas are great. Blindfolds are useful for all kinds of outdoor experiences.

Collecting Nets
Include large butterfly nets or small aquarium dip nets for fishing something out of a creek or catching a small insect.

Observation Pans
White dish pans are great but so are large margarine or whipped cream containers.

Hand Lenses
These don't have to be expensive. Hand lenses are handy if you have them on a string so students can wear them around their necks.

Measuring Tape

Thermometers

Compass
A compass is great for when someone asks, *Does moss really only grow on the north side of a tree?*

Flagging Tape
This is the stuff "tree people" use for marking which trees to save or cut. It comes in very handy for tagging objects to come back to later or for marking a temporary trail. You can buy flagging tape at a forestry supplier or hardware store.

Craft Sticks
Craft sticks work well for marking small discoveries in the ground as well as hiking trails.

Clipboards

Drawing and Writing Supplies
Include paper, pens, markers, pencils, crayons, and so on.

Nighttime Activities

any of the activities in this book can be successfully completed at night. However, those below are particularly fun to do after dark!

The White Sheet Trick

This activity is always a success! Rig up a white sheet with a strong light shining on it from the back. It won't be long before you start to collect literally dozens, if not hundreds, of insects. Capture a few to study, and then release them. While you've got the sheet up, you could also use it for silhouette skits. However, those same bugs could be a little pesky.

Bat Watching

Sit down and watch the night sky for bats. They're fascinating creatures. You could also have students play *Bats and Moths* (see page 17).

Night Bingo

Prepare Bingo cards using various night-sky attractions visible with the naked eye. Examples include: simple constellations, star clusters, the moon, Venus, a shooting star, the Milky Way galaxy, an airplane, and so on. Use an astronomy book to find enough items to fill a Bingo card. Students can then try to find everything on the card after dark.

Campfires

Campfires are always a hit. Try one with a theme or have one just for fun!

ABC Hike

Name: _____

A _____ B _____ C _____

D _____ E _____ F _____

G _____ H _____ I _____

J _____ K _____ L _____

M _____ N _____ O _____

ABC Hike (cont.)

Name: _____

P _____ Q _____ R _____

S _____ T _____ U _____

V _____ W _____ X _____

Y _____ Z _____

28

Scavenger Hunt List

Name: _____

As you (and/or your team) find and locate each item listed below, check it off. While you are not to collect the items, you must be able to certify that you actually found it, heard it, or saw it with your own eyes. Note: All items are "natural" as opposed to "human-made."

_____ feather

_____ maple leaf

_____ oak leaf

_____ seed

_____ something round

_____ something perfectly straight

_____ sign that an animal has been around

_____ something soft

_____ something useful to humans

_____ something camouflaged

_____ bird's nest

_____ something white

_____ something with a rough texture

_____ something blue

_____ something you could eat

_____ something that looks different in winter

_____ something that smells sweet

_____ something a rabbit might eat

_____ something we couldn't live without

_____ example of the balance of nature

_____ frog or toad

_____ bird

_____ eight-legged animal

_____ lichen

_____ plant with thorns

_____ fern

_____ something shiny

Adopt-a-Tree

Name: _____

Use this form to record your observations of the special tree you're adopting. Save these notes in your field journal or in a folder. You will return to this same tree throughout the year, so make your notes as complete as possible.

1. Locate your special tree.

2. Measure the circumference at the base and record. _____

3. Measure the circumference two feet (.6 m) from the base and record. _____

4. On a separate page in your field journal or on the back of this page, draw a detailed picture of the tree, showing its branches and general shape.

5. Draw a detailed picture of a leaf from the tree. Try to collect an old one from the ground. Do not pick a leaf unless instructed to do so by your teacher.

6. Make a rubbing of the bark pattern.

7. Look for signs of life on or around your tree. You will need to check the tree's "life zones," such as the roots, bark, lower branches, canopy, and so on. Note your findings.

_____

_____

8. Look for seeds your tree might have. Draw one.

9. Estimate the height of your tree. Record your estimate. _____

10. On a separate page in your field journal, sketch a map showing the location of your tree in relation to other large trees, rocks, buildings, and so on, that are located around it.

11. Smell your tree's bark. Describe it. _____

12. Estimate your tree's age. Record your estimate. _____

13. What makes you think your tree is this age? _____

14. How do you think your tree found this exact spot to take root? _____

_____

15. How do you think this tree might change by the next time you visit?

_____

16. Using a tree identification guide, what kind of tree do you think this is? _____

_____

Dinosaur Dig

Research Team Members:

_____

_____

_____

_____

Instructions:

Your team should work in one "dig grid" only. Dig carefully to make sure you don't damage any of your findings. Clean your artifacts carefully. Use available resource materials to answer the following questions.

1. To which grid were you assigned? _____

2. Did you find the complete remains? _____

3. What is the scientific name of your dinosaur? _____

4. How big does this dinosaur grow? _____

5. What does this dinosaur eat? _____

6. Where does this dinosaur live in addition to the grid where your team was digging?

   _____

   _____

7. Did you find any additional artifacts with the dinosaur remains? Describe them.

   _____

   _____

8. Additional Comments:

   _____

   _____

9. Resource(s) Used: _____

Sketch your findings on a separate piece of paper.

In the Dumps

Observation Record

Name: _____

Date of Initial Experiment: _____

What was buried or deposited? _____

_____

Describe the makeup of your "dump." Did you deposit natural materials (food waste, leaves, banana peels) or manufactured materials (aluminum cans, plastic bottles, plastic wrap)?

_____

_____

Where was this buried or deposited? _____

How deep was it buried? _____

How is it marked for reference? _____

Follow-up Observations

How long since it was first buried? _____

Observations (include what appears to be the same, what changes you have noticed, or if anything is missing):

_____

_____

_____

_____

_____

Continue to make observations on subsequent visits.

Chapter Two

Classroom/School Projects

Once you've tried your hand at the simple activities that begin this book, you can move forward to some programs designed to involve your students in more depth. Beginning on page 34 is complete information on starting a classroom nature corner or discovery center, including a humane way to have live creatures visit for a short stay in the "Class Menagerie."

Nature trails are wonderful ways for students to use science, writing, and math skills as they set about designing and building a variety of nature trails. You'll find information on the basics to get started in *Schoolyard Nature Trails*, beginning on page 36.

One favorite student activity is called *Waste Watchers*. This activity makes students aware of just how much food they waste. It can be used on a daily basis in a school cafeteria setting or during a special extended outdoor education experience held at an outdoor education center. All the information you need for this activity is provided in the section titled *Waste Watchers* on page 38.

Nature clubs are discussed on page 39, and a complete primer for hosting a student-run Earth Day Festival can be found in the *Earth Day Festival* section, beginning on page 40. There is a list of over 20 booth ideas, hints for student tour guides, a project outline form to help your students design and carry out their plans, and even a teacher grading checklist to help with assessment.

Classroom Nature Corner and Discovery Center

Students love to bring things into the classroom that they've found outside. However, students often hear, *That's nice, now take it back home—TODAY!* A classroom nature corner is the perfect place to display, save, and use all those wonderful discoveries students bring to school. If your school has room, you could even create a nature corner or discovery center!

How do you create a nature corner? To begin, send home a copy of the parent letter on page 43 to help solicit items. You'll be amazed at what people want to get rid of. In addition to asking parents and school families, ask around your school, other schools, local nature and science centers, and colleges. You might want to get a notice listed in your local newspaper. Just make sure you have room to store all the great stuff that will start arriving!

The following elements should be included in a well-equipped nature corner:

Resource Library

All kinds of nature books, field guides, how-to manuals, wildlife magazines, and so on, are a wonderful basis of an excellent reference section and lending library. Your discovery center library could also maintain files on teacher resources, web addresses, local and national environmental organizations, guest speakers, experts, and other area treasures. If possible, have a computer hooked up to the Internet for more in-depth research.

Nature and Science Equipment

Provide microscopes, hand lenses, bug boxes, thermometers, measuring tape, collecting nets and jars, and various tanks to be used as aquariums and terrariums. Also include all the items found in a Magic Bag (see page 25).

Interpretive Exhibits

As items come in, arrange them into content or concept areas. This could further lead to the development of discovery boxes (plastic tubs with lids), each containing a different theme. You might have one box on seashells, another on lichens, and one on rocks and minerals. The list is endless. Older students, parent volunteers, and other classroom assistants are good sources of help to serve as "docents" or "naturalists."

Class Menagerie

This is the "humane" way to care for all those living things kids like to bring in. Instead of setting up these helpless creatures in a permanent habitat, the Class Menagerie is a holding and exhibition space for a very limited stay—generally, three days or less. At the end of this time, the student who brought in the visitor agrees to return the animal safely home.

You may want to appoint a "naturalist-in-charge" to "check in" the visitor, record vital information, and then see that the animal leaves for a safe trip home. Use page 44, the *Class Menagerie Guest Register*, at the end of this chapter.

Schoolyard Nature Trails

Nature trails are a wonderful way for students of all ages to learn about nature. Any school can have a nature trail—even if it is located in the middle of a sprawling city! Nature trails can be wonderful class projects, club projects, a whole-school endeavor, or a parents association venture. However you approach it, a schoolyard nature trail can be a focal point of your school. Of course it can be used for science classes, but everyone can enjoy and benefit from this creation.

Basic Considerations When Creating a Nature Trail

Will the Trail Have a Theme?

Trails can begin and end with various "natural phenomena" highlighted with signs or markers, or they can have a theme. Themes can be changed each year or each semester so that a new set of students get the opportunity to build something or add to what another class has already started. If you have the space, leave each trail intact and add new trails from time to time.

Whispering Woods Trail

Theme possibilities include: habitats, succession, conservation and pollution, food chains, ecosystems, adaptation, and seasons. Be sure to include stops along the way to tune in your visitors' senses, such as "feel this bark" and "smell the richness of the dirt."

How Long Should the Trail Be?

A trail can be as short as 100 feet (30 meters) or as long as 1/2 mile (1 kilometer) or more. However, if a trail is too long, students may feel they have to race to get to the end. It is often better if trails are on the short side with fewer stops and attractions. This way, students will slow down and soak up their surroundings.

Where Should the Trail Be Located?

If you're lucky enough to be in a school near a forested area, you are very fortunate. But don't feel that only "woodsy" schools can establish and benefit from a nature trail. Your trail could be routed alongside the school building, taking into account the building's "natural features" such as shaded and unshaded sides; areas that are normally left unmowed, such as a fence line; cracks in a sidewalk; flower beds; a lone tree; bird baths; and areas where water is often present, such as around gutter downspouts.

Trail Stations

Trail stations are informative stops along the trail. Each station can emphasize a concept, tune in a sense, or reinforce some knowledge. While stops can be strictly informative, students will enjoy more and remember longer if there is some way to interact. This could be as simple as "Look behind you and count the different kinds of trees you see," or "Feel the bark of this tree." A word of caution—don't have too many stations. Having stations every few feet causes visitors to lose interest quickly. A rule of thumb is to include only about 10 to 12 stops on any trail.

You could also include a "nature's classroom" station along the route. This area needs to be large enough so the whole class can sit down for a group discussion or to complete some sort of project or investigation. A station like this makes a wonderful spot for journal or poetry writing, or for completing nature explorations.

Trail Signs

The easiest way to sign stations is to place numbers on a post and correlate this with a printed guide. Students can prepare professional-looking trail guides using a laser or ink-jet printer and any of the easy-to-use word processing or desktop publishing software that is available. Plastic or metal numbers can be found at any hardware or home furnishings store. Attaching these to wooden 4" x 4" (10 cm x 10 cm) pressure-treated posts will provide a fairly permanent and vandal-proof method of signing stations.

Some schools and groups sign their stations with all the information needed to explain each stop attached right to the post. The advantage here is that visitors don't have to pick up a trail guide to get started. There is also less waste, as most people don't recycle their trail guides, though there should be a box available for this at the end of the trail.

If you provide permanent signs, print them on hard card stock, laminate, and attach to a wood-backed post. However, these types of signs are the most prone to being carried off or knocked down. I suggest the "number on a post" system.

Naming the Trail

Most trail designers usually take into account a natural feature of the trail when naming it. For example, "Rainbow Creek Nature Trail" would be appropriate for a trail next to a creek with water that appears to be a different color each day.

Waste Watchers

Waste Watchers is an activity designed to make children aware of how much food is thrown away from their plates. Making people conscious of their food waste has the added benefit of saving money. Most wise food services will quickly stop serving what doesn't get eaten. Those that continue to serve food that kids won't eat are wasting someone's money. It could be yours!

How *Waste Watchers* Works

For this activity, use the chart on page 45 or design your own. You could have one column for each meal served or make a chart for each lunch of the week. Since measuring waste from an entire school could be quite unwieldy and messy, use a separate chart for each grade or class if attempting this on a school-wide basis. However, instigating a *Waste Watchers* program will be just the thing to slow or stop the waste flow.

Since you are measuring the waste from a child's plate, the old saying, *Take what you want, but eat what you take,* is appropriate in this case. If food is served cafeteria-style, then the child needs to say *no thank you,* if he or she doesn't want a particular item, or just ask for a "tiny bit" if he or she is unsure. Whatever children take but don't eat goes into the *Waste Watchers* can. A #10 tin can from the kitchen works well for this.

Don't count chicken bones and skin, eggshells, orange peels, apple cores, bacon fat, and countless other things students will test you with. Common sense dictates what's waste and what isn't. You might also not want to count things that come in single servings and the child isn't able to ask for a smaller amount. For example, if the kitchen is serving hamburgers and the child can't eat the whole thing, this wouldn't be counted as waste. If, however, the child has "eyes bigger than his or her stomach" and asks for two hamburgers and then only eats one, the second one gets dumped in the *Waste Watchers* can.

Measuring

With luck, you won't have to measure at all. But for those meals in which there is some waste, you'll have to devise a system of measuring. You can glance at the waste and compare it to the markings on the *Waste Watchers* chart and record the waste like a bar graph, stick a ruler in the waste, or even weigh everything to the gram.

Rewards

There really isn't any reason to reward no-waste meals. The excitement this activity generates usually is compensation enough. You can include "notes" on the *Waste Watchers* chart, showing levels of waste as encouragement. Extra recess for a week of "no waste" isn't a bad treat either!

Nature Clubs and Activities

Organizing a school nature club (or science/nature/environment combination club) is a great way to get students excited about nature and the environment in a more relaxed way than classroom projects. This is true even if the club meets during regular class time.

What Will the Club Do?

A club can have a specific theme each week, month, or cycle; or the club can happily explore whatever happens to be of interest. However, interest in attending nature club meetings will quickly wane if there's not much going on. For that reason, choose themes or projects that keep club members active, involved, and interested.

Possible Project Ideas

Recycling

Not only does this help the environment, but it can help your treasury as well. Recycle aluminum cans from across the campus and you could raise several hundred dollars a year! You can recycle paper, glass, or other items. Another way to encourage recycling is by starting a school or class book exchange.

Adopt Something

Clubs can have a great time adopting something. You can adopt a particular part of the school that needs "sprucing up," a nature corner that needs maintaining, or something more worldly like "Adopt-a-Whale" or "Buy an Acre of the Rain Forest" programs.

Start an Ongoing Project

Start a school nature corner, a wildlife feeding station, or a composting area. Build and install birdhouses. Plant trees. Host an Earth Day or Nature Festival. Encourage bicycling by sponsoring a Bicycle Safety Rodeo. Start an environmental newsletter to send to each classroom with ideas for saving the environment. (Be sure to print it on recycled paper.)

Study Something Special

The list of things to study is endless but can include animals of all types, ecosystems, gardening, freshwater fish, trees, wildflowers, or any other plant or animal in which your students are interested.

Earth Day Festival

Special festivals are shining ways to "spice up" the curriculum, create excitement, and increase awareness of whatever you're promoting—namely, taking care of our Earth. You may want to invite older students to run the festival, which offers lots of real-life educational benefits, including learning to plan, design, build, teach, and clean up. Equally beneficial are festivals sponsored by parent and/or teacher groups at your school, with adults running the activities.

On pages 46–48, you will find forms to help students plan their booths, and a sample grading form (if you feel you need one).

To help students go from booth to booth without missing any, you might try the "passport" idea. A passport is a card students carry with them from booth to booth. Pictured on the card is an environmental scene. As students go to each booth, passports are stamped with pictures relating to the scene (e.g., animal stamps), completing the environmental landscape. Students love getting their passports stamped, and it helps ensure that no booths are missed. Younger students especially love using passports. Have older students help "guide" the younger ones. Divide students into groups for easier manageability. Page 49 provides guidelines you can give to student guides.

Earth Day Festival Booth Ideas

Trash Bush—This is a "tongue-in-cheek" bush that has all kinds of trash attached to it. Each part of the bush (or tree) has an identifying label that refers to the kind of trash found around the campus. For example, a chip bag attached to one branch can be called a "baggius leftaroundia" and a soda can can be called an "aluminus eyesorious." This gets the point across that litter has no place on campus.

Nature Trail—This is a very short trail with only four or five stations that can be completed quickly with help from your student guides.

Solar Cooker—This will be a sure hit, especially if you're cooking solar hot dogs!

Composting Display—Make sure to put netting or a simple fence around your display.

Bird Feeders Made from Recyclable Materials—Have materials handy so visitors can make their own.

Art from Trash—This is a great way to use up some of the recyclables you have around school, as well as all those small bits and pieces of art supplies not quite large enough for a major project.

Bicycle Tune-ups—Promote self-propelled power as a means of making short trips by offering a clinic in bicycle tune-up and repair. A local bike shop may be willing to offer help in exchange for free advertising and exposure.

Make-and-Take Nature Art—Using objects found in nature, invite students to add a little glue, a little paint, and let their imaginations run wild!

Puppet Show or Short Plays—Invite students to put on a puppet show about an endangered animal or habitat, or about taking care of nature.

Recycling Skits

Paper Making

Clean Camping Techniques—Have a demonstration campsite setup and explain how to enjoy "no trace" camping.

Fruit Drying

Games—Ask adult volunteers to run a few simple, non-competitive games.

Quiz Show with Environmental Theme—Have students host a mini quiz show with an environmental theme. They can offer inexpensive prizes to everyone who participates, such as animal stickers.

Homemade Eco-Testers (Draft-o-Meter and Smog Catcher)—Have materials set up with take-home instructions so students can become "environmental engineers." The Draft-o-Meter is a 6" x 6" (15 cm x 15 cm) piece of plastic wrap taped to two pencils. When it is moved in front of doors or windows, a student can find air leaks. The Smog Catcher is similar but has a piece of waxed paper smeared with a thin layer of petroleum jelly. This device catches air-borne dust particles.

Bottle Biology—Invite students to create mini-terrariums out of recycled two-liter bottles.

Poster Contest

Astronomy/Constellation Sessions—Even in daylight, students will enjoy learning about constellations. You can make mini-planetariums for viewing constellations out of 35mm film canisters or old coffee cans with lids by punching small holes in one end in the shape of a constellation.

Endangered Species

Native American Legends—Invite a storyteller to tell stories, or students could act out some local legends.

Building Energy-Efficient Homes—Students can make models using shoe boxes, showing the effectiveness of solar energy and insulation.

Marine Biology—Recreate the effects of an oil spill disaster by dipping bird feathers in water-filled pie tins that have a few drops of motor oil added. Students are then instructed to clean the feather using a variety of detergents, towels, and so on. It isn't easy!

Nature Store—Open a "nature store" with all kinds of objects available for under one dollar. Include stickers, pencils, plastic hand lenses, and so on. This is also a good place to unload old classroom objects such as nature posters and field guides that are no longer needed.

Parent Letter

Dear _____,

Our class is creating a nature corner, and we need your help. We're collecting natural items of all types. Please go through your basements, attics, closets, and backyards for things that may be of use to us. Below are examples of some of the things we're looking for. This list is not complete, so additional ideas and objects will be appreciated.

- old microscopes, binoculars, telescopes
- old aquariums, nets, jars
- plant parts (bark, roots, buds)
- aromatic herbs
- lichens (plant fungus)
- nests (bird, wasp)
- preserved specimens
- archaeological objects
- various bones (cleaned and dried)
- turtle shells
- fossils
- nature sounds on CD or cassette

- snails
- compasses
- animal tracks in plaster
- tweezers
- surgical gloves
- complete skeletons (cleaned and dried)
- day packs/field packs
- plastic baggies
- X-rays
- wings, limbs, feathers
- plant presses
- field guides, nature books, wildlife magazines
- magnifying lenses

*Please be aware of any existing laws regarding the collecting and holding of natural objects before donating.

Thank you for your help and interest in your child's education.

Sincerely,

Class Menagerie Guest Register

Guest: _____

Habitat: _____

Check-In Date: _____

Check-Out Date: _____

Naturalist-in-Charge: _____

Where Animal Was Found:

_____

_____

Food Needed:

_____

_____

_____

Special Care Instructions:

_____

_____

_____

_____

Return Animal to:

_____

_____

Additional Comments:

_____

_____

_____

_____

Waste Watchers

	Day 1	Day 1	Day 2	Day 2	Day 3	Day 3	Day 4	Day 4	Day 5	Day 5
Try Harder!										
Could Be Better										
Not Bad										
Great!										

Earth Day Festival

Project Outline

Title of Booth: _____

Date of Festival: _____

Team Members:

_____   _____

_____   _____

_____   _____

Booth Description:

_____

_____

_____

Steps for Preparation:

1. _____

2. _____

3. _____

4. _____

5. _____

6. _____

7. _____

Materials Needed:

_____

_____

_____

_____

© Good Apple GA1688

Earth Day Festival (cont.)

Project Outline

Things to Buy: (Include estimated costs.)

_____   _____

_____   _____

_____   _____

_____   _____

People Who Can Help:

_____   _____

_____   _____

_____   _____

_____   _____

Plan of Action

(Rank-order what needs to be done by whom, and by what date.)

Priority	What Needs to Be Done	Who Will Do It	Date Due

Sketch: (Include booth plans, poster ideas, etc. Attach extra pages to this schedule.)

Project Plan Approval: _____   Date: _____

(teacher's signature)

Earth Day Festival

Student Booth Grading Checklist

Team Members:

_____ _____

_____ _____

_____ _____

Booth Name: _____

Your grade will be based on your team's work on the following items:

_____ Cooperative effort in class (15 points)

_____ Work completed in a timely manner (10 points)

_____ Each member has a part in booth presentation (10 points)

_____ Booth is attractive (15 points)

_____ Booth activity is informative (15 points)

_____ Materials are appropriate (15 points)

_____ Professionalism of presentation (10 points)

_____ Cleanup completed (10 points)

_____ TOTAL POINTS (100 points maximum)

Comments:

_____

_____

_____

_____

© Good Apple GA1688

Hints for Student Tour Guides

Follow the guidelines below as you lead younger students through the festival. Remember to set a good example, and most of all, have fun!

1. Your job is to help guide younger students around to all the booths.

2. Please stay with your group at all times.

3. Look for booths that are not crowded.

4. Make sure you take your group to each activity. You should plan to spend about 10 to 15 minutes at each booth.

5. When your group is finished with an activity, help students get their "passports" stamped.

6. Offer the booth leaders assistance (if needed).

7. Please set a good example by avoiding "horseplay."

8. If one of your group members needs to go to the bathroom, it's better to take the whole group for a bathroom break rather than send one child off alone.

9. If you're having trouble with a child who is "disruptive," please find a teacher to help.

10. If you find a booth that isn't interesting or exciting to you, please don't let your feelings show. Remember that someone has spent a long time preparing for this day, and your attitude can be the deciding factor to the booth's success for students visiting it. Please do your best to make this festival fun for your young charges and for the students in charge of the booth. You'll have more fun this way, too!

11. Enjoy the festival yourself, but remember that you're the leader, and the festival has been planned for the younger students.

12. If you have any questions, see one of the teachers in charge.

Chapter Three

Ongoing Environmental Programs

This chapter contains three activities that can be enjoyed during the entire school year. The basic ideas for all three programs are included, but you may customize the actual activities and time commitment to fit the needs of your students.

The first of these, *Earth Rangers* (see pages 51–53), was awarded the Gustav Ohaus Award for Innovative Approaches to Science Teaching. *Earth Rangers* helps students learn to be stewards of our planet. An important part of this program is the environmental project students choose to carry on as an ongoing activity. Examples include school recycling, anti-littering posters and skits, and adoption of an acre of rain forest.

The *Woodlanders* program (see page 54) and *School Outdoors* (see pages 55 and 56) are starting places for you to design programs of special interest to your students. *Woodlanders* allows you to pick and choose activities for small groups or even individual students as they work toward "Woodlanders Certification." *School Outdoors* is a name you can use for a special time set aside each week to try different outdoor activities.

Earth Rangers

Earth Rangers is a dynamic program for elementary school students, designed to open their senses to the natural world, instill a sense of ownership of their environment, and enable them to become better guardians of the earth. Earth Rangers "graduates" take great pride in their accomplishments. This program has been successfully used with students in grades kindergarten through fifth, and in 1994 was awarded a Gustav Ohaus Award for Innovations in Elementary Level Science Teaching.

Program Design

Earth Rangers is designed as an eight-session program, though it could be lengthened considerably by individual classroom teachers, or shortened if needed to fit into an existing curriculum plan. Each session lasts approximately 45 minutes.

Implementing the Program

The Earth Rangers program involves minimal requirements to implement and virtually no expense. Since all the "field trips" are held right on the school grounds, permission slips, bus fees, and extra chaperones aren't needed.

The activities and sessions on pages 52 and 53 are just guidelines. These activities can be supplemented with other activities to enable the program to mesh with any curriculum. There are numerous possibilities for making these activities cross-curricular, involving science, language arts, math, social studies, art, and physical education.

Earth Rangers is perfectly suited to a school in any setting—urban, suburban, or rural. The activities can take place on an asphalt playground, a grassy field, a wooded lot, or a sidewalk. Many of the activities can even take place indoors in case of inclement weather. The outcomes are the same regardless of where the activities are held—excitement and a new appreciation for the environment.

You may want to provide printed certificates for your Earth Rangers graduates. You can photocopy the certificate on page 57, or you may have certificates professionally printed. This should be the only money needed to implement the program, except for small miscellaneous expenditures needed for simple supplies. However, these supplies are most likely already in your classroom.

Earth Rangers Activities

The following session ideas will help you design your own *Earth Rangers* program.

Session One

The first session is designed to pique student interest. A serious tone is set, and "trainees" are told how tough it is going to be to complete the "training." Students are quick to accept the challenge and are soon ready to get to work. Explain that part of their training is learning to see things that most people miss. The perfect activity for this is *Last Detail* (see page 12). This activity teaches students to be observant of even the littlest things.

Session Two

Display a small "treasure chest" with a slit in the top. Tell students that the four "secrets of life" are locked inside. This instantly has them on the edge of their seats. Lead a discussion on what it takes to sustain life on Earth. Encourage students to offer ideas, while you list them on the board. Finally, as the suspense is at its peak, open the treasure chest. Pull out a vial of water and a small jar of soil, along with an explanation that oxygen and sunlight were in the chest all the time—entering through the slit in the top. Finish the session with a discussion of how important it is to protect each of these "secrets."

Session Three

Session Three is a "litter hike" activity. Have students go out in small groups armed with clipboards; pencils; and sheets listing several general forms of litter such as paper, plastic, aluminum, glass, and miscellaneous items. Invite students to find, collect, count, and record their findings. After about 20 minutes, have students return to the classroom to discuss their results. They will be amazed at how much litter they have found. Expand on these numbers in terms of the larger community—the neighborhood and the city. The numbers are staggering. When students finish this session, have them design a campaign encouraging others to care for the earth. You may want to brainstorm ideas for students' environmental campaign projects. Suggestions include: paper recycling, aluminum can recycling, adopting an area of the school to keep clean, or adopting a manatee.

Session Four

Session Four involves a scavenger hunt for natural items. There is no collecting in this activity, as caring for the environment means leaving natural things where they are found. After returning to the classroom, discuss students' discoveries and the important role each plays in the environment. Have students continue working on their campaigns.

Session Five

During the fifth session, read and discuss *The Lorax* by Dr. Seuss. This can develop into a sharing time in which everyone tells of someplace they know where people have cut down trees or where someone is polluting a creek. Discuss that sometimes there needs to be a balance between environmental and human needs for growth and development. For example, when cities grow there needs to be a balance between a place for people and a place for wildlife. Developers need to understand that there should be green places left when all the bulldozing is done so there is still a habitat for displaced animals.

Sessions Six and Seven

Sessions Six and Seven involve other activities designed to tune in students' senses to the environment. Go on micro-hikes, play nature games, listen for sounds, and look for signs of animal life. Students should continue working on their environmental campaigns.

Session Eight

Session Eight is both an ending and a beginning. In this session, discuss final plans for students' projects, and discuss the implementation and time frame. This begins students' real involvement as Earth Rangers. Finally, the certificates naming each student as an Earth Ranger can be presented. Students will be as proud of themselves as you are.

Invite students to display their *Earth Rangers* certificates outside the classroom door to let everyone who passes by know that they are working to protect the earth.

Woodlanders

 Woodlanders is the name for a group of activities designed to keep kids interested in the environment. Whereas *Earth Rangers* activities are designed to tune in a child's senses, these activities are more skill-oriented.

You could emphasize local natural history, include a certain number of sensory awareness activities, several nature activities, a couple of group dynamics activities, throw in some wilderness-outing skills, and anything else you feel is appropriate. When your students have completed a *Woodlanders* program, have an awards ceremony and present students with certificates (see page 58).

Woodlanders activities are designed to emphasize any aspect of the outdoors you wish. It is up to you how often and how long each activity should last.

For starters, here is a possible selection of *Woodlanders* criteria:

- Identify five local trees.

- Identify three wildflowers.

- Observe five signs of wildlife.

- Explain these terms: *habitat, adaptation, cycles.*

- List basic items needed to take on a nature outing.

- Complete two sensory awareness activities.

- Complete two nature activities.

- Complete two group dynamics activities.

- Share something you've learned with the group.

- Display a good attitude throughout the *Woodlanders* program.

School Outdoors

At least once a week, try and spend a class period outdoors doing a variety of outdoor education activities. This weekly session will quickly become a student favorite and is a wonderful way to close the week. It's also an excellent way to try new activities that may not fit into your general lesson plan.

Students can keep field journals of activities so there is continuity in the program from week to week. It's also easier for students to remember where you left off if something is written down. Field journals provide good practice in recording observations.

School Outdoors is a wonderful way to encourage students to write creatively. Their imaginations seem to soar when they're outdside. (You'll find more about using the outdoors to teach writing in Chapter Six.)

A good activity to start with is *Adopt-a-Tree*. This activity teaches kids to observe, measure, and record. They will come back to the same tree throughout the year to witness changes first-hand. Detailed instructions for this activity can be found on page 22.

Another good activity is map making. Map making works well after the *Adopt-a-Tree* exercise. Students begin by making a detailed map from the classroom to their special tree. They should include a "north" arrow as a reference point, using a compass for accuracy. Students should also include a starting point well-known to the class, such as "Go out of the classroom door into the courtyard and turn left." Students can provide details to make their maps accurate and understandable. Have them code the maps with numbers or symbols. This little "trick" makes the next step even more fun.

Redistribute the maps so each student has a map other than his or her own. The object is to locate the original cartographer's tree. This is often quite difficult and leads to excellent discussions on the need for accurate maps and directions.

Additional Activities for *School Outdoors*:

Plot Studies

Spend several class sessions studying the variety of habitats found on school grounds. For this activity, each student or student pair will need a simple piece of equipment to set boundaries for the plot he or she is studying. A hula hoop works well for this, but string also works as does a wire coat hanger formed into a circle or square.

Have students keep field journals of their findings, and date each entry. Urge students to slow down and do their very best work in observing, recording, labeling, and illustrating various study areas. Give students copies of activity page 59, *Nature Up Close*, to complete as they study their plot. Develop your own for other suggested study areas around your school. Make sure you spend time discussing what students have labored to record.

Study of a Lawn

Possible study questions: *How many kinds of plants do you see? What are the sizes of the plants? How many animals do you see? Describe the animals.*

Study of a Forest

Possible study questions: *How does the forest differ from the lawn? Draw and describe any ferns, mushrooms, or lichens you see. Are there any animals here? What is the temperature in the forest?*

Study of a Sidewalk

Possible study questions: *Is this sidewalk in the sun or the shade? Can you find any signs of plant life? Draw and label this plant life. Are there any signs of animal life? What is the temperature of your study area? Can you find a place where life (plant or animal) can get water in your study area?*

Nature videos, scavenger hunts, litter pick-ups, cemetery studies, poetry writing, and bird-watching are some more possibilities.

EARTH RANGERS GRADUATE

is recognized for completing various activities designed to protect our planet, and is hereby awarded the title Earth Ranger. Congratulations!

_____
(teacher's signature)

_____
(date)

THE WOODLANDERS PROGRAM

Congratulations!

_____ has completed a series of skill-building experiences to better appreciate how humans interact with the natural world, how to live in harmony with nature, and is now qualified to join the ranks of Woodlanders!

_____
(teacher's signature)

_____
(date)

Nature Up Close

Name: _____

Follow the steps below in order. Record all findings and illustrations in your field journal. This is not a race—take your time and make your entries as carefully and as accurately as possible.

Materials: hula hoop, field journal, pencil, hand lens, thermometer, collecting jar

1. Write today's date in your field journal.

2. Throw your hula hoop a few feet toward the study area so you'll end up studying a randomly selected site. This area needs to be separate from your classmates' study areas.

3. Observe your spot closely for five minutes. Make no notes during this time. Do not talk. Look closely at the area using a hand lens.

4. Take a temperature reading of your study area. Record the time and temperature in your field journal.

5. Make two lists. Label one *Living Things* and the other *Non-Living Things*. Under each heading, list all the examples you see in your plot for each column. Observe carefully and use a hand lens.

6. From standing height, draw a detailed illustration of your study area.

7. From an eye-level view, draw a detailed illustration as seen from that angle.

8. Label all illustrations.

9. Carefully capture an animal or insect living in your area using your collecting jar. Make a detailed drawing. Release the animal (insect) unharmed.

10. Be ready to share your notes with your classmates.

Chapter Four

Extended Outdoor Education Experience

This chapter helps fit the pieces of the puzzle together as you begin to implement an extended outdoor education program. You'll find a wealth of information, including where to find a site, how to staff the program, and when to hold it.

A complete detailed schedule of a sample four-day residential program begins on page 64. The schedule gives you activity ideas from the time students wake up until they go to bed. The program is completely adaptable and could be easily shortened or lengthened by adding additional activities from this book. Also included is a *"To Bring" List*, a *Student Contract*, and *Notes to Cabin Parents* (to help them feel comfortable as "cabin counselors.") You can find these forms on pages 73–75.

Implementing the Program

The only thing better than a classroom experience is an extended outdoor education program. *Extended* can mean anything from a half-day experience outside your classroom door to several days away from school. Your program can be held on the school campus, at a nearby park, at an overnight camp facility, or at an environmental education center especially geared for this type of program.

Choosing the Best Type of Experience

Whatever situation you feel most comfortable with will be best for you and your students. Many teachers feel better staying close to school, while others feel the urge to get away from the usual setting. In any case, the change of pace will be good and invigorating for both you and your students. The first step will be deciding on program goals and what you wish to accomplish.

Planning the Experience

The program schedule sample in this chapter can be adopted to just about any situation. It is based on the premise that you will be designing and implementing your own environmental education program and staffing it in-house. There are lots of advantages to running the program yourself. For starters, the program will be designed specifically for your class; the activities will relate to your curriculum; you set the time limits for each activity; and since you know your students best, you personally choose how best to wrap up each day as well as the whole experience. You can also bring your own traditional stories and "tricks" into the experience that you'll repeat from year to year. An important advantage to running the program yourself is the cost—you will save a lot of money!

Staffing the Program

Running the program yourself doesn't mean that you alone have to do all the work. Ask parent volunteers, a teacher's assistant, friends, and others who might be interested in getting a little fresh air. You could even hire a couple of professional outdoor educators to help run activities, and this is still a lot less expensive than going to an established environmental education center. You will want to prepare activity schedules, like those featured in this chapter, and meet with your "staff" to assign activities and explain how each is conducted. You may want to prepare any necessary materials for your facilitators, but they often will be willing to get everything together themselves. The first year will be the hardest, naturally. After that, it will get easier and easier.

Locating an Appropriate Site

Assuming that you are planning to run the program yourself, appropriate sites can be found everywhere. Day programs can be held at your school or a nearby city park. You can also look for a parent's or friend's country property, keeping in mind that you will need bathrooms and access to a phone for safety reasons. State and national parks are also great places to hold a program, but unless one is close, logistics might be unwieldy.

The Overnight Experience

The overnight experience is a favorite and will be one of the highlights of the school year for both you and your students. Planning an overnight experience takes considerably more time, but it's worth the effort. If you choose to go with an environmental education center, many of your tasks will be handled by them. However, letting them handle the details means you'll give up some, or all, of the originality of making the program truly your own. You'll likely participate in a program that's designed for all schools without your particular curriculum needs in mind. You'll also likely share the facility and staff with other classes, which isn't necessarily a negative. If the only way you can have an extended outdoor experience is if someone else takes care of the details, then the environmental education center is your best choice.

However, if you're planning to run your own program, there are thousands of summer camps in the United States, and many of them are anxious to have groups use their facilities during the school year. Most camps provide you with use of all the facilities, cabins for sleeping, and full meal service. If you're providing program staffing, fees are quite reasonable. Some camps will even let you bring your own food and prepare meals. This can save money, but the meal preparation and ensuing cleanup can be time consuming.

Summer camp names, addresses, and phone numbers can be found from parents, in the phone book, local Chambers of Commerce, and the Internet (use key words *summer camps* as a starting place). Also, the American Camping Association (ACA) publishes an annual directory of camps belonging to their organization. In addition to summer camps, check for area Y camps and church camps.

62

What Time of Year Is Best?

Any time you are willing to go is the perfect time! However, schools located in colder climates may want to go early in the school year or late in the spring. While many overnight facilities offer winterized accommodations, parents may be apprehensive about sending their children into the "wilderness" during the winter. You may want to consider the last week of April. This is far enough into spring to generally assure warm days (the nights can still be quite cold) and yet early enough in the school year to follow-up the program back in class with discussions and related activities. It's also late enough in the year to be considered the "ultimate culminating experience!"

Some schools like to start the year with a wilderness experience. Others may want to begin with a group dynamics overnight program that helps students learn to work together as a team. You can decide what's best for your class.

Terrific Tips

Bag of Tricks—Before heading out for your first extended outdoor experience, all good outdoor educators prepare a "Bag of Tricks" list. These are activities you can fall back on in case of rain or if something "bombs." Keep this list handy at all times and keep adding to it whenever you learn a new activity. One day, you'll be glad you are prepared.

Supplies and Props—Start an ongoing "Supplies and Props" list. Use this to note everything you'll need to run your program. Then, when the trip date gets near, you can split the list with other leaders and start collecting what you need to create a successful experience.

Getting Started

Following this introduction is the full schedule outline for fifth-grade "High Country School"—a four-day residential experience emphasizing environmental education. Since a camp property in the mountains is used for the experience, the different habitats this particular camp offers are studied, including forests, lakes, and streams. While this program is designed for four days, it could easily be adapted into multiple one-day programs, or simply reduced. By starting on Tuesday, you have Monday to use for last minute preparations, and then when the last day arrives, it's time for the weekend!

On pages 73–75, you'll find a *"To Bring" List* of items students should bring, such as clothing and supplies; a *Student Contract* (to help keep behavior in line); and *Notes for Cabin Parents.*

Sample Extended Outdoor Education Program

Following is a schedule for a four-day program. Improvements and fine tuning of the program occur each year as the curriculum changes and new ideas are introduced. As mentioned in the introduction, this schedule can be used as a starting place for your own extended outdoor education experience. Simplified activity descriptions are included below along with the schedule.

DAY ONE

9:00 a.m.   **Leave School**

10:00 a.m.   **Arrive at Camp/Introductions**

         Quick Review of Rules and Boundaries
         Move into Cabins
         Snack

10:45 a.m.   **Group Activity—Warm-up to Adventure**

         Stadium Entrance Cheer—Students make two lines similar to a tunnel that football players enter when being introduced. In turn, students are introduced by the teacher as the rest of the "crowd" cheers. It's quite a morale booster!

         Tag—Play several quick versions of "tag." This gets students warmed up. Rules are simple and everyone has a good time.

         Noah's Ark—This game is a great way to get cooperation rolling along. Also, it is quite funny to watch. (See page 21 for activity description.)

First Rotation

Interpretive Trails—Stream, Lake, and Pond

Place students into three groups. Each group will rotate to each activity. Each activity leader only has to prepare for one activity and will teach it three times. The activities you choose should be based on whatever you are studying. (The site for this sample schedule is located in the mountains and has access to forests, meadows, creeks, lakes, and ponds, so the activities lean toward those topics.)

Activities

A. *Stream Ecology*—In this activity, students observe, measure, and record things they find in a stream. They use dip nets and plastic wash tubs for collection. Emphasize to students that everything they catch or collect must be returned unharmed. Studying a stream often involves wading. Students love this. Discuss how life in the stream might differ from that in other water habitats you will study. (Have students complete the *Stream Ecology Study Guide Worksheet* on page 71.) A safety note: Make sure students wear shoes whenever walking or wading in any unknown waters, including streams and ponds.

B. *Hike to the Beaver Dam and Lake*—Students take a hike around the lake and look for differences between this habitat and that of the stream. It's fun for students to look for signs of beavers and discuss the pros and cons of having these mammals around.

C. *Habitats of the Pond*—Pond life can differ greatly from that of deeper and colder lakes, as well as from moving creeks and streams. Discussions with students can revolve around what makes a pond a pond and a lake a lake, why certain plants and animals prefer one to the other, and so on. Invite students to collect things by wading knee deep into the pond. This adds excitement and a touch of adventure!

1:00 p.m.   Lunch

After lunch this first day, introduce students to a couple of activities that will be ongoing throughout the four-day program. *Waste Watchers* is a standard for most environmental education centers (see page 38). End each meal with a clue in the *Mystery Passenger* game (see page 21).

The Discovery Wall, a long length of white paper taped to the dining-hall wall, is also introduced after lunch. As students find things and make discoveries, encourage them to record their findings on this chart. They can write poems, draw, describe, or even display some of their finds. This makes an excellent "take home" for the classroom after the program ends.

2:15 p.m.   *Second Rotation*

For the second and third rotations, try some of the group dynamics activities.

3:45 p.m.   *Third Rotation*

5:00 p.m.   Journal Writing and Silent Reading

This is time for a little rest. Have students write in their journals or read silently.

5:30 p.m. **Recreation and Relaxation (Parent Supervised)**

This is when parents arrive for the evening. They are on duty at this time to allow teachers and other activity leaders to rest. This is also a good time to prepare for the next day's activities.

6:00 p.m. **Dinner**

Waste Watchers and *Mystery Passenger*. (Repeat after each meal.)

6:45 p.m. **Quiet Games** (cards, board games, reading)

7:15 p.m. **Evening Program**

There are lots of program possibilities. You may ask a storyteller to entertain for an hour or so. But if you're ready and able to provide your own evening programming, here are some suggestions:

- skit night
- quiz show with environmental theme
- sing-along
- movie night (if the camp has a VCR)
- square dance
- astronomy session
- special guest

8:45 p.m. **Quiet Time** (get ready for bed, journal writing in the cabins)

9:30 p.m. **Lights Out**

DAY TWO

7:30 a.m. **Wake-up Call**

8:15 a.m. **Breakfast**

9:00 a.m. **Interpretive Trails—Mountains and Forests**

After spending the first day in and around water, groups will now spend time learning about forests and woodlands. Again, place students into three groups that will rotate to each activity.

9:00 a.m. *First Rotation*

10:15 a.m. *Second Rotation*

11:30 a.m. *Third Rotation*

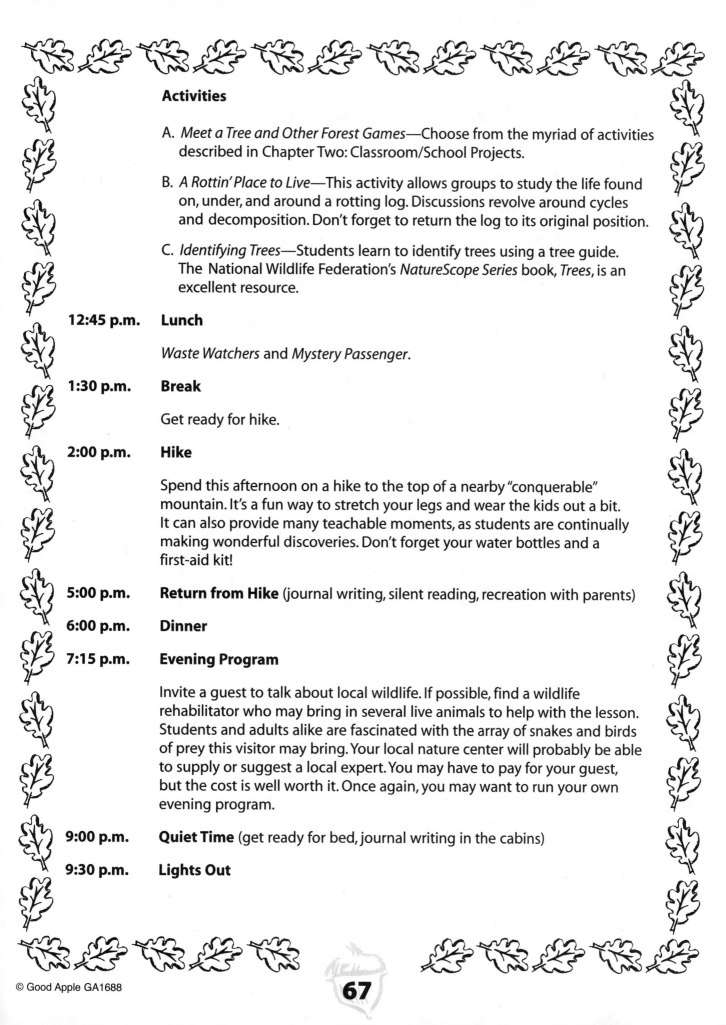

Activities

A. *Meet a Tree and Other Forest Games*—Choose from the myriad of activities described in Chapter Two: Classroom/School Projects.

B. *A Rottin' Place to Live*—This activity allows groups to study the life found on, under, and around a rotting log. Discussions revolve around cycles and decomposition. Don't forget to return the log to its original position.

C. *Identifying Trees*—Students learn to identify trees using a tree guide. The National Wildlife Federation's *NatureScope Series* book, *Trees*, is an excellent resource.

12:45 p.m.   **Lunch**

Waste Watchers and *Mystery Passenger*.

1:30 p.m.   **Break**

Get ready for hike.

2:00 p.m.   **Hike**

Spend this afternoon on a hike to the top of a nearby "conquerable" mountain. It's a fun way to stretch your legs and wear the kids out a bit. It can also provide many teachable moments, as students are continually making wonderful discoveries. Don't forget your water bottles and a first-aid kit!

5:00 p.m.   **Return from Hike** (journal writing, silent reading, recreation with parents)

6:00 p.m.   **Dinner**

7:15 p.m.   **Evening Program**

Invite a guest to talk about local wildlife. If possible, find a wildlife rehabilitator who may bring in several live animals to help with the lesson. Students and adults alike are fascinated with the array of snakes and birds of prey this visitor may bring. Your local nature center will probably be able to supply or suggest a local expert. You may have to pay for your guest, but the cost is well worth it. Once again, you may want to run your own evening program.

9:00 p.m.   **Quiet Time** (get ready for bed, journal writing in the cabins)

9:30 p.m.   **Lights Out**

7:30 a.m.	**Wake-up Call**
8:15 a.m.	**Breakfast**
9:00 a.m.	**Concept Paths**

Have students complete three high-interest activities, each designed to teach a different environmental concept. Again, place students into three groups.

Below are some sample activities, but your activities will vary depending on your site and what you are emphasizing in your program. You should find plenty of activities in this book to suit your needs.

9:00 a.m.	**Path One**
10:00 a.m.	**Path Two**
11:00 a.m.	**Path Three**

Activities

A. *Adaptation-Predator-Prey*—This is an OBIS *(Outdoor Biology Instructional Strategies)* activity that can be obtained from Delta Education. (See References on page 122.) *Adaptation-Predator-Prey* is a creative activity that invites students to design an adaptation for an imaginary creature to help it survive. Give each student a "challenge card" that says what his or her creature must be able to do or possess in order to eat and defend itself. Students then use anything they can find from the supplies you provide (glue, paper clips, rubber bands, paper cups, string, brads, craft sticks, natural items) to "build" their creatures. After the allotted time, have them present their creatures to the group.

B. *What's Your Range?*—This activity from National Wildlife Federation's *NatureScope Series* book *Mammals: Part One* is excellent for teaching the concept of "home range"—the idea that every living thing needs a certain amount of space to live. Have students begin by mapping their own communities, and then use this to compare with a variety of forest creatures.

C. *Web of Life*—This activity teaches students that everything in an ecosystem is connected to everything else. (See activity description on page 16.)

12:30 p.m.	**Lunch**

1:30 p.m. **Silent Walk**

Tell students that they are going to walk around the lake and choose their own quiet spots. They are to remain there silently until they are called for—approximately 45 minutes. During this time, they cannot talk to anyone, shout, or move from their assigned areas. Encourage students to use this time to write in their journals or as a reflective moment. Explain that there are very few moments in the day when everyone is expected to be quiet. This is one of them. Get students excited by explaining that wildlife might actually start nosing around once the kids have settled down.

2:30 p.m. **Blind Hike** (also known as *The Walk of Courage*)

After the *Silent Walk*, in which students have "tuned in" their senses of hearing and sight, take them two or three at a time on a special "blind hike." For this hike, run a long length of rope (about 100 feet, or 30 meters) over a course that students experience blindfolded. The rope has a starting and ending point, but in between goes up and down, around, over, and through various natural objects. Be sure the area is safe from obvious hazards. While three students take this walk at a time, separated from each other by a few feet, all are instructed not to talk. This, like the *Silent Walk*, is a quiet activity. Students who have completed this activity like to stay behind and watch, but they, too, are instructed to remain silent. To create more interest, have a breaking point where the rope suddenly stops and students have to grope around for the connecting piece in order to continue. While this connecting piece is only a foot (.3 meter) away, students start to get a little nervous when they can't find it. As simple as this activity seems, it offers students a whole new insight into what the natural world is like without the benefit of sight.

3:30 p.m. **Recreation Time (Parent Supervised)**

5:30 p.m. **Get Ready for Dinner**

6:00 p.m. **Dinner**

7:15 p.m. **Campfire**

Campfire is a traditional way of spending the last night. Even though it causes a few groans, you may not want to let students roast marshmallows. Thirty students waving around flaming marshmallows can be dangerous.

For this evening's program, you can have skits, songs, and journal sharing by both teachers and students. Traditionally, the campfire ends with a wonderful short story by Byrd Baylor called "One Small Blue Bead." This story is about courage, faith, and dreams expressed by an old man and a young boy in prehistoric times. The story begins when a present-day youngster discovers an old blue bead in the sand on the beach. He wonders where it

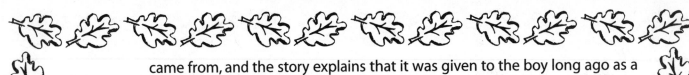

came from, and the story explains that it was given to the boy long ago as a sign of friendship. This story is used to present students with special blue beads as symbols of their experiences. The presentation of the beads is a highlight of the whole program, and often occurs after a student has shared something about his or her experience. Students proudly wear their beads for weeks after the program has ended. It is a fitting reminder of all that has been done and learned.

9:00 p.m.   **Quiet Time** (get ready for bed, journal writing in the cabins)

9:30 p.m.   **Lights Out**

DAY FOUR

7:30 a.m.   **Wake-up Call** (clean cabins, start packing)

8:15 a.m.   **Breakfast**

9:00 a.m.   **More Explorations**

The simple high-interest activities below are designed to "round out" the program. Like before, place students into three groups.

9:00 a.m.   *First Rotation*

9:45 a.m.   *Second Rotation*

10:30 a.m.   *Third Rotation*

Activities

A. *Natural Scavenger Hunt*—See page 20 for activity description.

B. *Map and Compass Basics*—Teach students the basic skills of using a compass. Then have them race against each other in a simple orienteering course.

C. *Group Dynamics*—There is just enough time for one challenging or two simple group dynamics activities. See pages 82–94 for suggestions.

11:15 a.m.   **Closing Ceremony**

Sharing Circle—Invite each student to share something about his or her experience. The topic is usually "What I Like Best About Outdoor Education." Page 24 lists other possible topics.

11:45 a.m.   **Finish Packing**

12:00 p.m.   **Lunch**

12:45 p.m.   **Depart Camp**

70

© Good Apple GA1688

Stream Ecology
Study Guide Worksheet

Name: _____

Things to do along the stream or creek walk:

1. Walk both sides of the stream. Find a safe place to cross with the leader.

2. Choose one section of the stream as your study area.

3. Measure and record the temperature of the stream in three different places.

    a. Place where temperature was taken: _____ Temperature: _____

    b. Place where temperature was taken: _____ Temperature: _____

    c. Place where temperature was taken: _____ Temperature: _____

4. Measure and record the stream's width and depth.

    Width: _____ Depth: _____

5. Estimate and record the velocity of the stream or creek by measuring the time it takes for a floating object (e.g., small stick) to pass from the beginning to the end of your stream section. Use general terms such as *moves slowly* or *moves swiftly*.

    _____

6. Look for signs of life (animal and plant) in your study area. With your leader's permission, you may want to collect some of the things you find. These should only be plants and animals that can be returned without damage.

7. On another sheet of paper or on the back of this page, draw pictures of the items you've collected. Using a field guide, identify some of your findings.

8. How are the plants and animals in the stream different from those in the lake or pond?

    _____

    _____

    _____

    _____

Forms to Get You Started

"To Bring" List

This list describes everything students, parents, and other volunteers will need to bring for a four-day program. It also mentions a few "don't brings." It is helpful to send this list out at least three times—the first time about three weeks before the program, then about ten days before, and finally a couple of days before you leave. Discuss the list in class a few days before leaving.

Student Contract

Using student contracts is a good way to help you avoid a cabin of kids staying up half the night goofing off. For a one-night program, a contract is especially needed. Generally, students will be so excited about this trip that they won't sleep for nights beforehand. Chances are they won't sleep the first night of the trip either. While a contract does help, keep in mind that it's hard to control enthusiasm. Extended trips have the added benefit of having enough time and nights for students to get into some sort of routine. They will eventually go to sleep.

Notes to Cabin Parents

Parents are often reluctant to sign up to spend a night or two in the cabins with students. They start to panic as time draws nearer, especially when they realize that there might be six or seven boys or girls in their group. This sheet helps them understand exactly what is expected of them. This program is a great experience for parents. It not only involves them closely in their children's education, but also helps them appreciate teachers that much more!

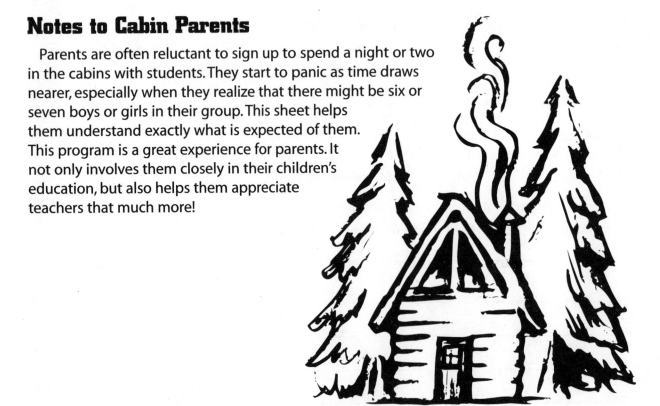

"To Bring" List

Clothing

- Bring clothes for four days, including some extras. (All clothing should be old and ready for hard use.)
- Set of "swamp clothes"—old clothes you don't mind getting muddy, wet, or dirty. Make sure you have an old pair of shoes you can wade in.
- Spare pair of shoes
- Rain gear and some sort of rain hat
- Bandannas (2)
- Some clothes for cooler weather

Equipment

- Day pack
- Water bottle
- Sleeping bag
- Pillow
- Bath towel and hand towel
- Personal grooming items
- Flashlight

Other

- Journal
- Pens and pencils
- Book(s) to read during quiet time
- Medicines (if needed)
- Small non-electronic games for free time
- Sunscreen or sunblock
- Sunglasses
- Laundry bag
- Insect repellent

Don't Bring

- Knives of any kind
- Food of any kind
- Any other "doubtful" items

Student Contract

In order for your outdoor education experience to run smoothly, all students and parents are asked to sign this agreement. It is important that students understand the necessity of following safety rules and rules designed to make this experience comfortable and worthwhile for all participants, including students, teachers, parents, program staff, and camp staff.

It is also understood that a student who refuses to follow these rules and standards will not be allowed to continue his or her participation in the outdoor education program. Parents will be called to come and pick up a student whose behavior is a detriment to the program or whose disregard for safety rules is a danger to himself or herself or the rest of the students, teachers, or staff.

1 You are to abide by all safety rules as stated by the camp owners and by the school staff and additional outdoor education staff.

2 You are expected to participate fully in all activities unless you have been excused by the teachers.

3 You must be ready to participate in each activity at the announced time. Being ready means being dressed properly and having the necessary equipment (e.g., field journals, pencils).

4 You must stay out of all camp buildings and facilities unless specifically given permission to be there.

5 You may not visit any cabin other than your own.

6 You are not allowed to be near the lake or creeks without being with the school group during an activity.

7 Quiet times are to be observed as such. There will be no loud talking or other excessive noises during these times.

8 Bedtime is when you start settling down for the night. All students are expected to go into a "quiet" mode at bedtime and help with the calming down process. No screaming, shouting, or being out of the cabins will be allowed once students report to cabins for the evening. Your cabin counselor will set the exact moment for "lights out," and at that time there will be no more talking.

_____   _____
(student signature)   (parent signature)

Notes to Cabin Parents

Thank you for agreeing to serve as a cabin parent for our outdoor education program! We encourage you to arrive in time for dinner, which will be served around 6:00 p.m. Otherwise, you may arrive anytime, but we'll definitely need you at camp by 9:00 p.m.

In the Cabin

* For some students, cabin time will be the "highlight" of their outdoor education experience. Imagine, a sleepover for 30 kids! The good news is—you'll only be in charge of around seven.

* Plan on giving students 30–40 minutes to settle down, brush their teeth, put on their pajamas, and so on. You need to set the tone for the evening by not allowing them to shout, scream, climb in the rafters, jump on bunks, or be out of the cabin.

* "Lights out" needs to occur after this 40-minute period. After this time, students need to be quiet.

TIP #1—You are encouraged to read to students using a flashlight. Please bring something with you to read, but avoid ghost or horror stories. Otherwise, you may find seven wide-eyed youngsters up all night trying to climb into your bunk!

TIP #2—If you end up with a bunk that seems to sag to the floor, you might find it more comfortable to place your mattress on the floor itself. It helps!

Wake-up Call

* Wake-up call will be at 7:30 a.m., with breakfast at about 8:15 a.m. Exact times will be announced the evening before. Students should have something to read by his or her bedside if he or she wakes up early. Do not allow students to leave the cabin before the wake-up call.

* After the wake-up call and before breakfast, students need to clean the cabin. On the last day, the cabin should be left clean with all items accounted for. Students should leave their belongings in the cabin. They'll retrieve them when it is time to leave.

Breakfast and Beyond

* Your "official" duties end at the beginning of the breakfast period—approximately 8:15 a.m. You are invited to eat breakfast with us, but if you must leave early, you are free to leave after your group has cleaned the cabin.

Chapter Five

Group Dynamics

This chapter contains dozens of activities and additional variations designed to help your students learn to work together as a group both in small teams and as a whole class. Group dynamics activities teach students problem-solving skills, communication, teamwork, compromise, and trust. To begin, you'll find five steps to help you get started. Most of these activities involve very little preparation, and many activities can be adapted to indoor spaces in case of inclement weather.

This chapter includes a myriad of group dynamics activities ranging from simple to complex. All of the activities are challenging. However, students will quickly learn that things go better when they listen to each other.

There are several quiet games beginning on page 93 that ask students to work together as a team. This section ends with a short simulation activity called *Stranded*. Students are asked to choose 15 items and place them in priority order, indicating which they would need in order to survive if they were stranded in the wilderness. This activity helps students learn the skills needed to reach a consensus.

The chapter ends with a complete plan for an extended group dynamics program called *The Cornerstone Experience*. Beginning on page 100, you'll find detailed information for setting up a two-day program that emphasizes teamwork. It's a perfect way to start the school year. An hour-by-hour schedule is also provided on pages 102–105.

The What and Why of Group Dynamics

What Are Group Dynamics?

Cooperative learning has been an educational buzzword for years. After all, it makes a lot of sense to help students understand that it's better to work together. Students will most likely work with other people all their lives no matter what their chosen occupation. The sooner a class bonds, the sooner you can get down to the real business of teaching and learning.

Group dynamics activities (sometimes called "group initiatives") were around long before the term *cooperative learning* became a buzzword. Outdoor educators have always used these types of games as a way of "breaking the ice" with a group, and are excellent for teaching a variety of skills, values, and concepts. You'll recognize many of the games and activities as ones you've played since childhood. But what sets group dynamics activities apart from everyday activities is what is done with the knowledge learned while playing the games, and the follow-up at the conclusion.

The activities in this chapter help you reach teamwork goals. Some are fast-paced, some are quiet, many involve physical activity, others involve problem solving—all, however, require heavy doses of thinking.

Why Group Dynamics?

There are several reasons why it is important to lead students through activities designed to help them work together as a team. Even if you only accomplish one or two of the skills and values you're after, you're that much ahead of where you might have been without these activities. And since you and your students will really enjoy this change of pace, it's worth the effort!

Group Dynamics Activities Teach . . .

- Trust among team members
- Problem-solving skills
- Self-confidence
- Communication
- Teamwork
- Leadership
- How to be a good follower
- Decision making
- Compromise

The Basics of Facilitating Group Dynamics

Most outdoor educators use a certain protocol when running group dynamics activities. This is what sets these games apart from those played simply "for fun." Follow the steps below when facilitating group dynamics games and activities.

Step 1

Set the stage. This often involves making up a story about a situation in which the only way to come out of it "alive" (or at least in one piece) is to complete the game to the leader's satisfaction. There is a goal, and this goal can only be reached with the cooperation of the whole group. Invent your own stories. Make them as silly as you wish—students will love it! (They'll remember the story, even if they forget parts of the game.)

Step 2

Provide the rules. The rules for games can be simple or quite complex. Once you set the rules, students must complete the game accordingly or they haven't reached their goal. So, if you say, *You must get your whole group across the poisoned peanut-butter field without letting go*, and the group lets go, then they need to start over. It can be frustrating, but the challenge is still there. When they make it, everyone will feel exhilarated. If they don't make it, this can lead to an excellent discussion afterward, beginning with, *Why didn't you make it?*

Step 3

Do the activity. After setting the stage and listening to all the rules, kids will be chomping at the bit to get started. Let them begin. Offer no suggestions. Give no clues. Be merciless. They need to solve these problems on their own. If they mess up, they start over. If they argue, they settle it themselves. There is only one thing they can't do—give up. Encourage them to try again, to try something new, listen to someone else's idea (perhaps someone who hasn't said a word all day, or all

year!), or rethink the whole problem. This is when you start to see class leaders emerging. Sometimes the student who never says much in the classroom will come up with the best solution. What a wonderful breakthrough!

Step 4

Add modifications. After the initial attempt, or successful completion, of the activity—it's time to add modifications. It might be adding a time limit for a second round, or you could try to increase or decrease the number of feet (or meters) a group has to move or the number of people who must be involved. You can say that everyone has lost their ability to talk or you could blindfold the leaders and make them speechless, if necessary. All of these modifications help make an activity more challenging and interesting. By "handicapping" your class leaders, other students are given the chance to shine and take over leadership roles.

Step 5

Debrief. This is a very important final step in the activity and one that is often overlooked and forgotten—especially in the euphoria of the moment. Possible points to discuss

include: *How did it work? How did you solve the problem? What was causing the breakdown? Was everyone listening? Did some leaders emerge? What was the major obstacle to overcome? How did you feel when you couldn't speak? Could you do this better next time? What could you do to make it work better next time? What did you learn about yourselves? What did you learn about the group? Are you ready to try again?*

Using Group Dynamics in the Classroom

You could spend a day playing these games and have a wonderful experience. You could very faithfully complete the five steps for each game with the knowledge that you've worked out "some problems." But one of the real values of group dynamics activities is that you can use what you and your students learned through these experiences throughout the school year in the classroom.

Subtle comments or reminders can do wonders. When a group is arguing about something, when no one is listening, or when the whole class seems to be falling apart, it's time to recall some of your "debriefing" from the activities. You could say something like, *Remember last month when we were doing the* Tin Can Pass *and you couldn't get the can around the circle? What did you do to solve the problem?*

Remind students that life is like these games—more gets accomplished when everyone listens, when we try other people's ideas instead of "shooting" them down, when we are willing to let others speak, and when we search for solutions instead of placing blame. Group dynamics activities are a great way to encourage students to learn the value of teamwork and cooperation. These aren't just "games."

Standard Props

Most of the games in this chapter are simple to play and involve little or no props. They require some advance preparation, but most of it is reading and understanding the activities themselves. You'll find the activities easier to facilitate with each new attempt. Only those activities that don't involve intricate setup or time-consuming prop building have been included. Most everyone is knowledgeable about "ropes courses" these days. They are wonderful additions to a school program and have a lot of merit in the outdoor education field. Ropes courses need to be built, inspected, and certified by professionals, and facilitators need extensive training to make sure the activities are handled properly and safely. Most classes would benefit from participating in a ropes course program at a facility set up for that purpose. The activities presented here offer much, if not all, of the same value without the expense.

You will need some basic props. Chances are you probably have everything you need right now somewhere in your school. Basic props include:

- blindfolds (bandannas work well)

- "soft" balls of all types and sizes (tennis, Nerf™, beach)

- several hula hoops

- nylon cord, string, and rope

- plastic buckets

- paper and pens

- stopwatch

- chart paper and markers

An Acknowledgement

Since the 1970s, Karl Rohnke and his organization, Project Adventure, have been well known in the field of group dynamics, ropes courses, and outdoor education. Teachers and other game leaders interested in learning more about this area of outdoor education are advised to read his incredible resource books. See References, beginning on page 122, for a list of excellent, user-friendly books by Rohnke and Project Adventure, as well as other suggested reading.

Group Dynamics Activities (Simple)

These games have been selected for their simplicity, minimal equipment requirements, and quick preparation time. They barely scratch the surface of available games that meet the above criteria. Likewise, there are hundreds more games that involve only slightly greater equipment needs and preparation time. Use the Resources section, beginning on page 122, as a starting place for developing your own games treasury.

Most of these games can be played indoors or out. However, most of them produce a lot noise! Warn your neighbors if these games are being played inside.

Finally, in many of the more challenging games, there are no definitive solutions. As long as the team is following the rules you've stated and comes up with a way to solve the problem, it is successful. Many times when these games are played, students will come up with new, and often better ways of solving problems.

These games are even more meaningful when you play them right before something students really want to do—like eat! For example, tell groups they can go to lunch only when they have solved the problem you're about to present. It helps them get right to work. It's important that each group ends with success. If it seems that a group is never going to succeed with a particular activity, leave time for a debriefing session. You'll want to dissect the team's dynamics, and see if you can come up with reasons why they weren't able to finish. Or, you can choose an activity you know all students can complete successfully.

Ice Breakers

Hug Tag

Equipment Needed: none

This game is a variation on "tag" with a unique twist. Players must "hug" themselves into a particular-sized group when that number is called. In other words, if a leader yells *four*, a player must end up in a group with four people. A round lasts just long enough to see if each group has the right number. Then, it's on to the next round with another number. This game is also fun when you call out numbers in a foreign language or throw in a little math. It's fun to end the game with the total number of students in the class. Nothing quite beats seeing 36 people involved in one giant hug! You can also call out *one*, and everyone hugs themselves.

Triangle Tag

Equipment Needed: none

This is another fast-paced game of chase, but in this version, it involves a little cooperative help. Divide students into groups of four. Three group members hold hands, making a triangle; the fourth person is the "chaser." One of the three in the triangle is the "target." The chaser's job is to tag the target, while the three in the triangle, including the target, must prevent the chaser from doing so. The triangle must not let go of hands, so their means of protecting the target from the chaser is to turn left or right faster than the chaser can tag. All three members of the triangle must work together to protect the target. Once a chaser is successful, he or she becomes the next target.

Energy Relay

Equipment Needed: bandanna, chair, coin

This is a good game for when you want to demonstrate the negatives of too much competition. This game can be complicated, but it's worth it!

Two teams will compete against each other. Have each team line up and hold hands (throughout the game). Teams should be parallel to each other, about three feet (.9 meter) apart. Choose one end of the two lines to be the starting point, and you (or an appointed coin flipper) wait at that end. The other end of each line extends to where you've placed the bandanna (or other object) on a chair between the two lines. The action starts at the other end—the end with the coin flipper.

Here's what happens: Everyone watches the coin flipper. The students at the head of each line are especially alert. The coin flipper flips the coin, catches it, and covers it with his or her hand. Then, the coin flipper uncovers the coin to reveal heads or tails. If the coin comes up tails, nothing happens. If the coin comes up heads, each end "beginning" student squeezes the hand of the person next to him or her. That squeeze gets passed on to the next person, and the next person, and so on down the line, until the "ending" students receive the squeeze. The first student feeling the last squeeze reaches out and snatches the bandanna, and one point is scored for his or her team. After a point is scored, the two beginning students move to the other end of the line so the next people in line are now first, and become the coin watchers. Continue with this rotation until everyone has had a chance at both ends of the line.

This is supposed to be a quiet game. No one should talk. While this never happens, you'll soon be able to point out that being quiet and concentrating will pay off with big dividends in this game—similar to life.

What happens if one (or both) coin watchers squeeze and the coin came up tails? (This happens all the time.) Hands should only be squeezed on "heads," but many coin watchers are so excited that they squeeze anyway. Once the squeeze starts its journey down the line, it can't be called back. This should be obvious since no one is supposed to talk. However, there are usually groans coming from the coin watchers who squeezed inadvertently. When the bandanna is picked up, assuming the squeeze came on a "heads" toss, the team picking it up forfeits a point to the other team. It's kind of ironic that when both teams squeeze prematurely on a "tails" toss, the slower team actually wins! Continue the game until everyone has had the chance to be a coin watcher, or until a specified number of points has been reached.

Remember to remind students throughout the game that its purpose is to teach teamwork. They'll be attempting to place blame on someone just as soon as their team picks up the bandanna when they should have left it alone.

Variations: Have everyone keep their eyes closed except the two coin watchers and the two at the other end getting ready to snatch the prize. Or, if you're into math, you could make this game academically challenging by subtracting numbers from the team that squeezed when it wasn't supposed to and got the bandanna. Teams could eventually end up with negative numbers.

Hula Hoop Pass

Equipment Needed: two or more hula hoops, stopwatch

This zany activity provides plenty of laughs! Begin by having the group make a large circle and hold hands. Have two students break hands just long enough to slip their hands through one of the hula hoops. Then start timing as the group sees how long it takes to get the hoop passed completely around the circle without breaking hands. It takes a lot of contortionism to get the hoop up and over each student, and those on either side of the hoop will need to help with maneuvering.

Variations: After trying this once or twice with one hoop, try adding a second hoop. The second hoop should go in the opposite direction. At some point, the hoops will need to cross each other. Continue to use your stopwatch as a motivator. You could also blindfold a couple of students, who will need instruction from their classmates.

Impulse

Equipment Needed: stopwatch

This game is similar to the *Hula Hoop Pass*, but involves passing energy along like in the *Energy Relay* (see page 83). Have students hold hands in a large circle. Instead of passing the hoop from person to person, they pass a squeeze. Time them, and try to beat records for how quickly the energy can get passed around the circle.

Variations: Try having the first person squeeze both of his or her hands. Then the energy is being passed in both directions, and the person somewhere in the middle is going to be quite busy. Another variation is to add a "yell" or "special sound" when you feel the squeeze. This is another good way to get out some excess energy.

Data Processing

Equipment Needed: stopwatch

Students become human computers as they attempt to solve a series of directions of ever-increasing complexity. You might allow very young students the luxury of talking, but I always keep older students (third graders and up) silent. The rules are simple. You state a problem, and students need to solve it without talking. You will be timing them to see if they can beat the "world's record." After the data processing has finished, stop the watch and do your accuracy check. Reveal the time.

Example Problems:

- Line up in order of height from shortest to tallest.

- Line up in order of height from tallest to shortest.
  (This one is great because inevitably, most students will act before thinking. The simplest, and thus quickest, solution is for students to remain where they were after the original command. However, most groups will run around starting all over. It's then fun to see who "thought" about staying put, but was compelled to move when the line broke up.)

- Line up in order of shoe size.

- Line up in alphabetical order by last name.

- Line up in order of birth month. (This usually takes some "sign language.")

- Line up in order of birth month and day. (This takes lots of "sign language"!)

Variation: Blindfold several students.

Moonball

Equipment Needed: beach ball

This game is a little like volleyball. The object is for the entire group to keep a beach ball in the air by hitting it up like you would a volleyball. However, in volleyball, you only have three hits before putting the ball over the net. Here, there's no net and no team. The object is to keep the ball in the air for as many hits as possible. A good number to start with is 50. This seems simple enough, but there will be too many ball hogs or over-zealous ball hitters to keep the ball in play. Students quickly learn the wrath of their fellow classmates as they start to tone down and become team players. Once 50 is reached, increase the goal. You might also want to say that no one can hit the ball twice in a row.

Find Someone Who ...

Equipment Needed: prepared worksheets, pencils

This is a good no-pressure game to help students get to know each other. Prepare worksheets with lots of "incomplete" statements pertaining to students, such as *plays tennis* or *is bilingual*. These statements all have to start with *Find someone who ...*. Students will have to go around and see which classmates fit these "descriptions." If you have new students and can do some research, it's great to be able to include some statements that only pertain to them. This forces the established class members to talk with the "new kids on the block." A simple example might be *Find someone who is new at school this year.*

A sample *Find Someone Who ...* worksheet can be found on page 95. Use it for most groups as is, or adapt it to the age and specifics of your group.

Once you distribute the worksheet, explain that students will sign their names on the lines next to the "appropriate" statements on their classmates' sheets. You can decide whether a student may sign his or her own sheet. You might consider letting students sign their own sheets just once. Also, you may want to limit any one student from signing more than two statements on a classmate's sheet. This forces more interaction by everyone.

Group Dynamics Activities
(A Little More Complicated)

Tin Can Pass

Equipment Needed: #10 tin cans

In this game, teamwork, not speed, counts most. Have students stand in a circle, shoulder to shoulder. Then have them sit down with their feet stretched out toward the middle. Place a can on the outstretched legs (at the ankles) of one student. The object is to pass the can completely around the group without dropping it. Students can only use their legs and feet to pass. It won't take them long to figure out that they can alternate between using their feet to pick up and pass the can from one person to the next by placing it inverted over one foot.

For the next round, you might say that the can must stay upright. To make it even harder, add some tennis balls to the can. Then for the challenge of all challenges, add water. Students love it! They also learn that the goal is for the can to get around the whole group, and neighboring students will often lend their feet to the cause.

Variations: Blindfold several students. Now they'll be completely dependent on classmates to see that the can is passed successfully. But remember, the can must touch each person's legs as it makes the pass. It's especially challenging to blindfold several students sitting next to each other. You could also require that the only help they can receive must be verbal or from classmates seated to the right and/or left of them.

Group Juggle

Equipment Needed: soft juggling items such as Nerf™ balls

Start by asking students how many of them can juggle. Generally, you'll find a couple of kids eager to "show their stuff." Explain that by the time you're finished with this activity, every person will be able to "wow" crowds with his or her juggling ability.

Have students make a circle, facing inward. The circle should be large enough to leave room for tossing and catching, but not so large as to make these distances impossible for the average student. Give one juggling item (ball) to a student. That student then tosses it to someone across from him or her. The student who catches the ball tosses it to someone else. Students continue tossing the ball until everyone in the circle has caught it once. Students need to remember who they throw the ball to and from whom they receive it.

When one rotation has been completed, let students practice it a couple more times. Remind them that whenever they get a ball, they always throw to the same person and receive from the same person.

Once students have mastered the art of throwing, they're ready for juggling. Start adding additional balls by giving one to any member of the group or to the original starting person. As each ball is added, it gets thrown to the next person in the rotation. Try three balls, then four. Before you know it, everyone's juggling!

Another challenge is to suggest that students complete one round of the juggle (with one ball) in under two seconds. This will seem completely impossible, but reviewing the basic rules—everyone must move the ball in the original order—opens up to interpretation how exactly the ball can be moved from person to person. Students will come up with all types of solutions and eventually, someone will come up with an answer that everyone agrees follows the rules to beat the two seconds. There's more than one way to accomplish this. See if your students can figure out how.

Hint: Tell students to use only underhand throws. Suggest that they initially throw the ball to someone across from them rather than on each side or in close proximity. If someone misses a catch, no problem. This student should just wait until the next ball comes his or her way and then put it in play. And if someone catches another student's ball, this player should throw it to his or her usual receiver.

Variation: New classes or groups that don't know each other can benefit from also having to call out the name of the person to whom they are throwing. This can help students learn each other's names a little faster.

Knots

Equipment Needed: none

This is a perennial favorite and involves no equipment except arms, hands, and legs. Divide the class into groups of approximately five to six students. Ask students in each group to make a small circle, facing each other. Have them extend their hands inward and use their right hand to reach over and take another person's right hand. Then have them place their left hand in and take someone else's left hand.

To make this work a little better, suggest that they not take the left and right hands of the same person, and they shouldn't take the hands of the person adjacent to them.

After "hand taking" is complete, instruct students to untie themselves from this "human knot," or pretzel, without letting go. In almost all cases, it can be done. Students just need to be patient and caring. They will need to coach others about where and how to step through or over various bodies to get untied. Occasionally one group will untie themselves, but one or more members will be facing outward. This can still be considered a successful mission.

Lap Sit

Equipment Needed: none

This game involves lots of teamwork, and the more people, the better! Everyone stands in a circle, shoulder to shoulder. Then, have them turn to the right. It helps to have your group close up the circle a little bit by taking a small step inward. Everyone then places their hands on the hips of the person in front of them. On the count of three, have them slowly lower themselves into a lap-sitting position. The weight is evenly distributed (more or less), and everyone ends up having his or her own "chair"!

Insignificant "I"

Equipment Needed: none

This game is quite simple, yet can also be frustrating. It truly points out that there's a whole world of people out there, not just students. Have your group make a circle large enough so everyone can see each other. Then, without forming a pattern and without any instructions, have everyone take turns stepping into the circle and "numbering off," beginning with *one*. Each student decides when to step in and say the next consecutive number. The very second two students step in at the same time and/or say a number at the same time, the whole process starts again with someone stepping in and saying *one*.

This sounds a lot easier than it actually is. Remind students that there can't be a pattern. In other words, it is against the rules to just go around the circle counting off. This game truly takes patience and involves everyone realizing that they aren't the most "significant" person in the game, class, or world. That's a hard concept to swallow, but a good lesson to learn.

Super Glue Shoes

Equipment Needed: none

This game offers an unlimited number of solutions and is easy to implement. Divide your class into groups of about six students. Have groups line up with each student placing his or her right foot next to the next person's left foot, and that person's right foot next to his or her neighbor's left foot, and so on, until everyone in the group is lined up with feet touching. Each group should line up on the same starting line. Explain that some strange super-powerful glue has stuck their feet together! Then tell them they have to walk a distance of 15 feet, or 4.5 meters, (you decide the actual distance) without "breaking" their feet apart. Students will try all kinds of methods, and you can decide on what you'll allow. However, their feet cannot be tied together.

The Shuffle

Equipment Needed: low curb/bench/log

This is a great activity to do with the accompaniment of dramatic music. Place students in teams of 12 or so, and have teams stand in a straight line, on a curb, 4' x 4' (5 m x 5 m) length of lumber, bench, or log.

Once the group is assembled, inform students that they are crossing a treacherous bridge when one end of the line comes to a locked gate. The good news—they have a key! The bad news—it's attached to the wrist of the person at the far end of the line! The object is

for each group member to switch places with the person in the exact opposite position in line. For example, when the game comes to a successful conclusion, each student will be in the exact opposite place in line as he or she was in the beginning. If there is an odd number of students in the group, the center person stays put. How students move is up to them, but one thing they can't do is fall off the "bridge." If one person steps down, all students must start over again in their original positions.

Bog Cross

Equipment Needed: several hula hoops

Students have a terrible situation on their hands—they need to get the entire group across an alligator-infested bog without falling in! The bog is at least 75 feet (23 meters) long, and the only way they can cross is by stepping into (not out of or on) hula hoops. It seems hula hoops have magical life-saving properties.

As many people as can fit into a hoop can safely reside there, but they have to get the entire group across the bog. The idea is for the group to figure out that they'll have to throw a hoop down, get as many people into that hoop as possible, then toss another hoop onto the ground. The first group will need to move into the second hoop, then into the third, and so on, until they've reached the safety area. You need just enough hoops so that one or more can be sent back to the starting point. It takes a few attempts before students realize that hoops cannot get so far apart that they can't be shuttled back to the beginning. If someone steps on or outside of a hoop, the group must start over.

Ships and Sharks

Equipment Needed: several hula hoops

In this game, students attempt to cross a "shark-infested ocean". The game begins with small groups of students (but large enough so that fitting them all inside a hula hoop is difficult) holding onto the rim of a hoop. They then move across the "ocean" until you call out *shark!* Once students hear this, they start moving across the ocean by running or walking and holding onto the rim of the hoop. When they hear the dreaded "shark" warning, they throw down their hoop and all jump inside. If any group member is not inside the hoop by the time you count to three, or if one member steps outside or on the hoop, that group must go back to the starting line and begin again. By the way, there are a lot of sharks in the water!

Don't be bashful about giving the "shark" warning. Continue play until all the "ships" have made it safely to the other shore, a distance of at least 150 feet (46 meters).

Blind Polygon

Equipment Needed: blindfolds, long piece of rope or string

This simple game helps students develop leadership skills. The group starts in a circle, with all members blindfolded. Have students hold onto a length of rope which has been tied into a loop. Call out geometric shapes for the group to form. For example, square, rectangle, triangle, pentagon, and so on. No one is supposed to talk, and each student should have at least one hand on the rope at all times. After the group thinks it has formed the perfect shape, the leader lets students remove their blindfolds. Discussion with students could center around such questions as *Why did you decide to take charge? Did you (the group) think this activity would be possible? Why was this frustrating?*

Hint: Eventually, someone will decide to take over the leadership role in this activity and personally take charge of placing people in some sort of position to form the requested shape. However, that person isn't supposed to talk or let go of the rope.

Stand Up/Bottoms Up

Equipment Needed: none

In these activities, student pairs of similar size attempt to help each other stand from a sitting position. There are several variations. In *Stand Up*, students sit back to back and link arms behind them. Then, by carefully pushing against each other and against the floor, they attempt to stand up. You could add a third and fourth person to the original pair for even more fun!

In *Bottoms Up*, two students sit facing each other. They put their feet against each other and start putting pressure on the bottoms of their feet. Their hands are behind them on the ground. The object is to exert enough pressure so that both students are able to raise their bottoms off the ground.

The All Aboard

Equipment Needed: hula hoop, 2' x 2' (.5 m x .5 m) platform

This is one of those classic activities in group dynamics that is usually associated with a set of group initiatives and low ropes course elements. This one is included because you can do it using minimal equipment. The object is to have your whole class, or as many students as possible, squeeze themselves into a small, defined space. That space could be the area inside a hula hoop. You could also mark an area on the classroom floor or playground with chalk. This activity is often done while standing on a 2' x 2' (.5 m x .5 m) platform that stands a couple of feet (.5 meter) off the ground. When done in this manner, it takes some very careful spotting and holding. Even with students crowding into a small space on the ground, it is still important that they know they must hold on to and support each other.

Variation: Try blindfolding students.

Quiet Problem-Solving Activities

Wordles

Equipment Needed: index cards, pencils

Wordles are those wonderful common phrases depicted with short words or letters placed in strategic locations. Prepare a set of about 20 wordles on index cards for each team. Show an example or two on the board, and then instruct each team to work together to solve as many wordles as they can. Explain that in most cases, more brains will be better than one. At least that's what you're hoping to prove. After time is up, reassemble the class, hold up each card, and ask for the answer. You can keep track of correct answers if you want. There are plenty of books available with wordles. Here are a few examples:

man overboard

she's beside herself

space program

Happy Landings

Equipment Needed: blindfolds

This game is great for teaching skills in giving and receiving directions. Most of the class serves as buoys while a few others will be "natural sea-going obstacles." To play the game, one student finds him- or herself shipwrecked and blinded. This student wears the blindfold. Luckily, a bystander on the shore witnessed the disaster and is going to try to bring the blinded sailor to safety. The blinded sailor is able to hop aboard a one-person life raft and row through all the obstacles to safety. The sailor must depend on careful directions from the witness who is standing on the opposite shore.

The blindfolded sailor starts at one end of the playing area and walks (rows) to the opposite end as the witness calls out directions. The rest of the class serves as buoys and other obstacles by gently swaying back and forth in the "bay." If the blinded sailor bumps into any obstacle, the raft goes down, and he or she is lost at sea. (Caution your buoys to sway gently.)

Compliment Cards

Equipment Needed: 5" x 8" (12.5 cm x 20 cm) index cards, pens/markers, tape

This isn't really a problem-solving game, but it is an excellent way to end a series of group dynamics activities. Start with a discussion of what a compliment is, and of course, what it isn't. Then use tape to attach an index card to the back of each student. Ask students to go around to each classmate and write a sincere compliment. They can sign or initial their compliments or remain anonymous. After everyone is finished, invite students to remove their cards and read what others wrote about them. This is, and should be, a "feel-good" activity.

Hint: If someone absolutely cannot think of a compliment for a particular student, then it is best for that student to write nothing. However, if several students are purposely avoiding another student, you will need to intercede. You can write your own compliment on that person's card and specially ask some other trusted students to do the same.

Problem-Solving Scenarios

Equipment Needed: none

There are plenty of wonderful group problem-solving scenarios that ask students to make some "life-saving" decisions. The challenge of these activities is coming to a group consensus. Class members will quickly learn the art of discussion and compromise.

Stranded (A Project Adventure Problem-Solving Activity)

Directions: Give students copies of the *"Stranded" Problem Sheet* (pages 96 and 97). Ask them to choose 15 items to keep and eliminate 14 they believe are not necessary for survival. Then, have them rank the 15 items in order of importance. After students have finished their rankings, place them in groups of four to seven. Ask the groups to compare their rankings and reach a consensus (i.e., form a group list that satisfies all members). Explain that consensus does not mean that everyone agrees unanimously. Rather, it is a way for group members to come to agreement through compromise.

Scoring: Give students copies of the answers on pages 98 and 99. (These answers were determined by the experts at Project Adventure.) Students can come up with a score by keeping track of how far off their answers are from those given by the experts. For instance, if an item is ranked as two, and Project Adventure has it ranked as eight, the difference is six. The same difference would exist if the item was ranked by students as 14. As in golf, the lower the score, the better. The scores provide a useful basis for discussion, and it is also interesting to see if individuals did better than groups as a whole.

Find Someone Who . . .

Name: _____

Was born in March _____

Has twins in the family _____

Plays tennis _____

Rides at least 30 minutes to school _____

Has at least four pets _____

Is bilingual _____

Has lived in or visited a foreign country _____

Plays a musical instrument _____

Is the only kid at home _____

Doesn't like to dance _____

Is the middle child _____

Has a summer birthday _____

Has two brothers or two sisters _____

Likes to read mysteries _____

Can stand on his or her head _____

Has been to Alaska _____

Has a mountain bike _____

Doesn't like hot dogs _____

Plays on a sports team _____

Is new at school this year _____

"Stranded" Problem Sheet

Name: _____

The Situation

On vacation in July, you and your family have been traveling through the wilderness of western Maine in a pickup truck with a camper. In a blinding rainstorm, you made a wrong turn on an unmarked lumber road. You have wandered more than 150 miles (241 km) over a maze of lumber routes into the wilderness. Your truck has run out of gas and now you, your parents, a ten-year-old sister, six-year-old brother, and the family cat are lost.

After a family conference, you decide it is not wise to split up. You are going to try to walk back together. You are pretty sure that if you pace yourselves, you can cover about 15 miles (25 km) a day. Because of the remote area in which you are stranded, there are no helicopters or jeeps patrolling the area, and you have seen no other cars or houses.

Your family is dressed in lightweight summer clothing and sneakers. Temperatures at night drop down into the low 40s. It is also bug season. As you look around, you pull some items out of the camper, some of which may be useful.

The Task

You must choose, and put in priority order, the 15 most necessary items for survival in the wilderness. The others can be eliminated.

_____ fishing gear (hook and line)

_____ $500 in traveler's checks

_____ four sleeping bags

_____ matches

_____ steak (3 lbs., or about 1 kg)

_____ marshmallows (four bags)

_____ bug repellent

_____ walkie-talkie

_____ road map of Maine

_____ 5-gallon (about 23-L) water jug

_____ instant breakfast (three boxes)

_____ house and car keys

_____ cigarettes

_____ two-burner stove

_____ family tent (10 lbs., or 4.5 kg)

_____ snake-bite kit

_____ alarm clock

_____ five cans of kidney/liver cat food

_____ 5-lb. (about 2-kg) tub of peanut butter

_____ bathing suits

_____ 10-lb. (4.5-kg) cheese wheel

_____ transistor radio

_____ 5-foot (1.5-m) tent pole

_____ sheath knife

_____ wool sweaters for everyone

_____ raft paddles

_____ inflatable rubber raft (two pieces, 20 lbs., or 9 kg)

_____ paperback books

_____ first-aid kit

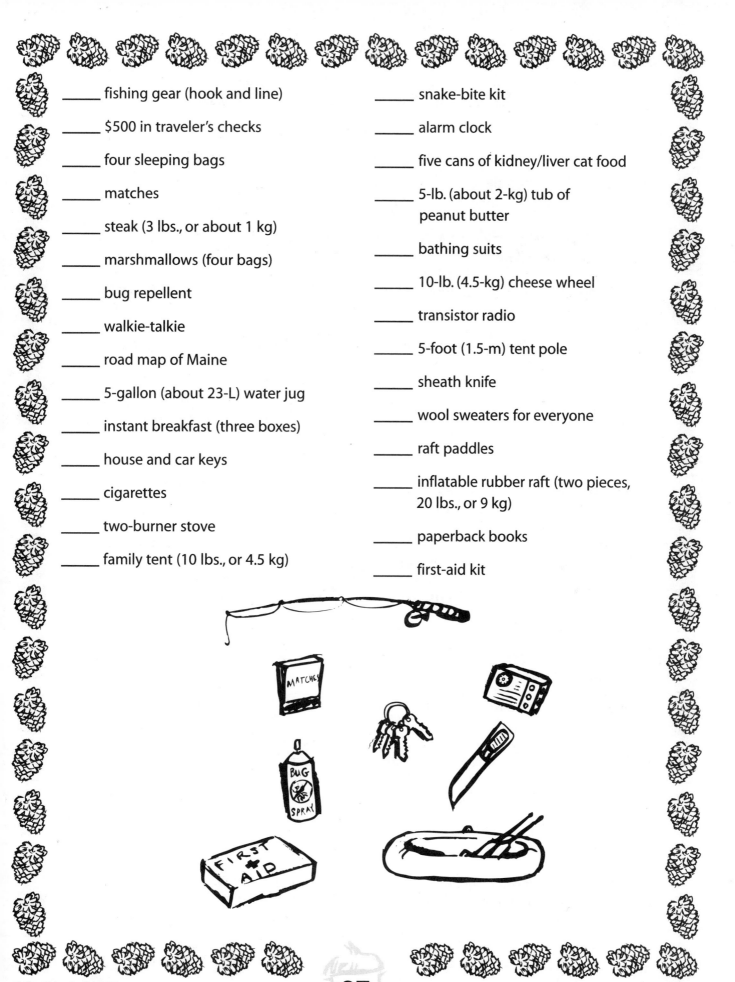

Reproducible

"Stranded" Answer Sheet

The following items should be kept for survival:

1. *Bug repellent*—In early summer, the bugs in Maine are so fierce and can bite people so badly that their eyes become swollen shut.

2. *Four sleeping bags*—Full rest and warmth are essential to survival, as humans can live 30 days on stored fat.

3. *Tub of peanut butter*—Each tablespoon (15 mL) of peanut butter contains 100 calories and is high in protein.

4. *Cheese wheel*—Cheese provides calcium and fats, and is an easily digestible source of protein.

5. *Steak*—Steak is a good morale booster, semi-perishable, and should be eaten promptly, as it is mostly protein.

6. *Instant breakfast*—This is a lightweight source of vitamins and protein.

7. *Kidney/liver cat food*—This is a valuable, if somewhat unappetizing, source of protein and fat; protein lasts longer than any other nourishment in providing energy.

8. *Matches*—Fire may be necessary to dry wet gear, boost morale, make a signal fire, and prevent serious hypothermia. It could also be used to keep away animals.

9. *Tent*—This can be rigged for use as a place to keep warm and dry, to keep bugs out, or to carry equipment in.

10. *Sheath knife*—A knife is useful for preparing any captured animals, such as frogs, or cutting strings, food, a pole, and so on.

11. *Road map*—A map may be useful for sighting major landmarks like lakes, rivers, and so on.

12. *Wool sweaters*—These will provide lightweight warmth, wet or dry.

13. *First-aid kit*—Bandages, aspirin, and petroleum jelly may be useful for minor injuries.

14. *Transistor radio*—The family can tune in for radio programs about a search for them or for weather forecasts.

15. *Fishing gear (hook and line)*—This may provide a supplementary source of food. Or the line may be used for tying up supplies.

The following items are *not* necessary for survival:

Marshmallows—These are not necessary, but could be a possible morale booster.

House and car keys—These items are lightweight, but not useful for survival.

Traveler's checks—Traveler's checks are nice to have, but not necessary for getting out of the woods.

Clock—For survival, it is not necessary to know time.

Walkie-talkie—It will not carry any useful distance.

Snake-bite kit—There are no poisonous snakes in Maine.

Paperback books—These weigh too much to be useful.

Bathing suits—These are not necessary clothing items.

Rubber raft—A rubber raft is too heavy, and also not likely to be useful.

Paddles—These are no use without a raft.

Two-burner stove—A stove is too heavy, and wood fires can be used instead.

Tent pole—The knife can be used to cut a pole.

Water jug—The water in the Maine wilderness is potable.

Cigarettes—Cigarettes are bad for your health.

Additional Comments

This problem is not appropriate for all parts of the country. However, a similar situation can be devised that allows students to have "unqualified expertise" about local wilderness conditions, enabling them to find a common solution. This activity is quite old, and when it was written, a lot of drinking water in the wilderness would be considered potable. However, it is now advised that all water in the wilderness or back country be treated before drinking. That could change the ranking somewhat, or you could explain that the family could treat all their water with iodine tablets found in their first-aid kit or by boiling the water before drinking it.

* Stranded is used with permission of the author, Karl Rohnke, and comes from Cowstails and Cobras: A Guide to Ropes Courses, Initiative Games, and other Adventure Activities. See References at the back of the book for complete information.

Extended Group Dynamics Program
The Cornerstone Experience

An overnight experience at the beginning of the school year is often a great way to teach students how to work together as a class, to cultivate them to work and trust their teachers, and get to know everyone better. It's also a lot of fun!

Needless to say, a program like this is best done at the beginning of the year. Some schools hold these types of programs during the very first week. Others wait a few weeks. Students may be ready, but many of their parents are not.

Another reason for holding a program like this so close to the beginning of the school year is so those important follow-up activities can be enjoyed throughout the rest of the year. A big dose at the beginning can work wonders, even magic, on your class. You'll get to learn how your students react to a variety of situations (both positive and negative), how they solve problems, where natural groups form within the class, and how new students are fitting in.

The program described in this chapter is called *The Cornerstone Experience*, and there is no reason why it can't be enjoyed at school during the school day. There is, however, something invaluable in an overnight experience. Being with your students for a 36-hour period (or longer) can be an eye-opening and completely worthwhile experience. You may discover a side of your students that isn't often visible during the normal school day. Hopefully, in all cases, it will be a positive side you're seeing.

About *The Cornerstone Experience*

The schedule for this program runs over two days. It can easily be adapted to a one-day program or multiple part-day programs. (See page 62 for ideas on locating appropriate sites.) If you want to work with your students first-hand, you will want to create your own program. However, use parents for nighttime cabin supervision.

Most of the activities are specially planned for adaptation to indoor or outdoor play. Your students will be so excited about this experience that they'll be terribly upset if it is called off because of inclement weather. Simplified activity descriptions are included in this agenda. Your activities may differ greatly from those used here. Be creative!

Refer to pages 73–75 for a *"To Bring" List, Student Contract*, and *Notes to Cabin Parents*. (While teachers run all the activities, you will want to ask for parent volunteers to provide cabin coverage at night. You do need some rest.)

The name *Cornerstone* is used to suggest a starting place for the school year. Use these experiences as building blocks for everything that will occur during the next nine months. It can become a tradition, and most likely, the name *Cornerstone Experience* will stick.

The Cornerstone Experience

DAY ONE

9:45 a.m.   **Arrive at Camp**

Introductions
Quick Rules
Cabin Assignments

10:00 a.m.   **Baggage Brigade**

Students' belongings are generally in the back of the bus. What better way to unload them than with this activity! It is reminiscent of an old-time fire brigade, except that you will be moving baggage instead of water. Have students make a line extending from the back of the bus to a place where you can stack and sort baggage. Tell them they are going to move the bags from the back of the bus by handing them off, one piece at a time, to the next person in line. The last person will then stack it at the end where it can be reclaimed later. Explain that if even one piece of luggage touches the ground on its way, the entire load has to be repassed back to the bus, and they must start over.

Let the bus driver know ahead of time that this activity might take ten minutes or an hour and ten minutes. If the driver absolutely can't wait, you could unload all the luggage into one pile and then have students move it down the line to the end pile. This is just as much fun, and just as effective. However, if you get your driver a large cup of coffee or two, I'll bet he or she will enjoy the performance.

10:15 a.m.   **Find Cabins, Get Settled**

10:30 a.m.   **Program Orientation: "Why We're Here"**

Review class rules, i.e., *Everyone has a right to be heard; No put downs; Mind the Golden Rule;* and so on. Set your own guidelines for this discussion, but be sure to discuss that this experience is supposed to be fun for everyone and it's important that everyone learns to work together.

11:00 a.m.   **Get Acquainted Activities: Warm-up to Fun!**

Have a list of activities available for most time slots. Do an activity as long as it seems enjoyable or until you have accomplished the set goal. Any activities that are omitted may be played when time exists later in the program. (Note: Many of the following activities are described in detail elsewhere in this book. Otherwise, a description is included here.)

A. *"Everybody's It" Tag*—This is a quick game of tag in which everyone is "it." This is often called the world's quickest game of tag, especially if you bring in the boundaries. Once you say *go*, kids start running around tagging other kids. Once a kid is tagged, he or she is out until the next round. This will usually take about 40 seconds.

B. *Triangle Tag*—This activity requires some cooperation. (See page 83 for activity description.)

C. *Hula Hoop Pass* (see page 84)

D. *Impulse* (see page 85)

E. *Hug Tag* (see page 82)

F. *Meet Your Friend*—This is a good way to end this first session. Pair each student off, preferably with someone other than his or her best friend. Ask them to spend ten minutes finding out things about each other that the class may not know. When time is up, have each student introduce the other and tell the class something interesting about him or her.

11:45 a.m.   **Cornerstone #1**

The theme of a "cornerstone" is used throughout this program. For each of these, have a short class discussion on a particular theme. Sit in a circle so everyone can see each other. Emphasize that one person talks at a time, and that there are no wrong answers or comments. Everyone is entitled to an opinion. Explain how a cornerstone is considered one of the most important pieces of a building's construction, and that's why everyone is here—to help lay the groundwork for a successful school year. Hold "cornerstone" meetings at the same place so students will associate that spot with serious dialogue.

Cornerstone discussions, while important, aren't meant to be boring. Run them for only a few minutes. Generally, the conversations are quite lively. Use topics appropriate for your class—this schedule only provides suggestions.

Topic: "Treat People and the Environment with Respect and Consideration"

12:15 p.m.   **Break—Get Ready for Lunch**

12:30 p.m.   **Lunch—Introduction of *Waste Watchers*** (see page 38)

1:15 p.m.   **Group Initiatives**

The following games work well during this time slot.

A. *Find Someone Who . . .* (see page 86)

B. *Tin Can Pass* (see page 87)

C. *Super Glue Shoes* (see page 89)

D. *Energy Relay* (see page 83)

2:15 p.m. **Cornerstone #2**

Topic: "Competition—Too Much of a Good Thing?"

This is a great topic for the second cornerstone meeting because students just played *Energy Relay*—an activity that can bring out the worst in competition. This is a good time for a meaningful discussion on the positives and negatives of competition.

3:00 p.m. **Group Dynamics Activities**

A. *Noah's Ark* (see page 21)

B. *Bog Cross* (see page 90)

C. *Ships and Sharks* (see page 91)

4:00 p.m. **Work on Skits for Performance**

Divide the class into small groups and tell them they'll be performing a short skit after dinner. Leave the topics to them, although you could have a theme. However, skits should be "acceptable" to everyone. Working on skits is definitely a team-building experience. To maximize this benefit, groups should include a "mix" of students, avoiding known cliques.

5:00 p.m. **Cornerstone #3**

Topic: "Friends—Making Them/Keeping Them"

6:00 p.m. **Dinner**

6:45 p.m. **Quiet Time** (reading, journal writing, practicing and preparing for skits)

7:30 p.m. **Cornerstone #4**

Topic: "Cooperation—Getting Along with Classmates and Teachers"

8:00 p.m. **Skits and Songs**

8:45 p.m. **Snack**

9:15 p.m. **Sharing Circle: "Something I Learned Today"**

9:30 p.m. **Bedtime**

DAY TWO

7:45 a.m.   **Wake Up, Cleanup, Pack**

8:30 a.m.   **Breakfast**

9:15 a.m.   **Group Initiatives** (Groups will switch after 40 minutes.)

        A. *Group Juggle, Knots,* or *Lap Sit* (see pages 87–89)

        B. *The Shuffle* (see page 90)

10:45 a.m.   **Cornerstone #5**

        Topic: "Goals for the School Year"

11:15 a.m.   **Individual Goal-Setting for the Year**

        Students write goals, both personal and academic. These are collected and saved to use as reminders throughout the year.

12:00 p.m.   **Lunch**

12:45 p.m.   **Final Sharing Circle: "Something I Learned in This Program"**

1:15 p.m.   **Closing Statements**

1:30 p.m.   **Load Vehicles**

2:00 p.m.   **Depart**

Additional Comments

As with all extended programs, it's a good idea to develop your own "Bag of Tricks" (see page 63). When one activity isn't working and you've exhausted those on the schedule, you'll have some extra activities ready to go. Any activities you don't get to during a scheduled time can automatically be placed on your "Bag of Tricks" list for later use. If you never get to some activities, you can always try them later during *School Outdoors* (see page 55) or some other time you need a break.

Hint: Never distribute the program schedule to kids. They get too worked up over times and titles. The schedule is just a loose time frame for leaders. Also, having a printed schedule helps assure parents you know what you're doing!

Chapter Six

Reading, Writing, and the Great Outdoors

The "great outdoors" has always been inspiring to writers, the famous and the amateurs. What is it about being in the wilderness, or even our own backyards, that inspires thoughts and feelings? It could be the many wonderful sounds, the smells, or the way the wind blows through our hair—but whatever the reason, you'll find the outdoors will inspire your students like nothing else can!

This chapter begins with several ideas that can't help but give students something to write about! Full details are provided for how a teacher can combine children's literature with the outdoors by participating in "My Side of the Mountain" Day. Jean George's classic novel, *My Side of the Mountain*, is the theme of this wonderful day spent outdoors recreating the adventures of the book's youthful protagonist.

Finally, you'll find two short stories to tell around the campfire or in the classroom. These stories each have a message students will long remember.

Using the Outdoors to Teach Writing

Have you ever faced a class of young writers and have one, or all of them, mention the words *writer's block?* Even students who have never succumbed to that problem berfore will often jump to get aboard the band wagon if it gives them a good excuse not to write. Taking your students outdoors and letting them experience a whole new world will often provide them with a fresh new variety of writing topics.

Almost any new activity will give students plenty to write about, including a total immersion activity. A total immersion activity is one in which the participant gets completely caught up in something new or out of the ordinary. It might be a fairly commonplace activity in which he or she has never participated or something rather ordinary seen from a new perspective.

Once you've orchestrated the activity, it's time to get students writing. They should begin the initial phases of writing right away while images are still fresh in their minds. While your students might complete their writing a day or two later in the classroom, the pre-writing, brainstorming, and webbing should take place at that moment. Below are some possibilities for memorable experiences sure to inspire even the most reluctant writers.

Activities Requiring Little Preparation

- *Blind Hike* (see page 7)
- *Hundred Inches (250 Centimeters) Hike* (see page 7)
- Environmental awareness activity that asks students to see something from a different viewpoint, such as *observe the ground from an ant's perspective*
- Any group dynamics activity involving problem-solving skills
- Any kind of hike out of the classroom

Activities Requiring More Preparation

- Ropes course, wall-climbing, or rock-climbing experience
- Overnight camping experience
- Caving
- White-water rafting

Combining the Outdoors and Children's Literature

There are plenty of excellent children's books that lend themselves to incredible outdoors adaptations. Jean George's *My Side of the Mountain* is nice in the winter for capable readers, and a whole day's worth of activities related to this novel are listed beginning on page 111.

Background

My Side of the Mountain is a children's classic about a boy, Sam Gribley, and the year he spends living on his own in the mountains. Spending a day recreating the life and times of Sam Gribley becomes a dream come true for students as they find out what it might have been like for Sam to survive in the wilderness without parents, siblings, or teachers.

"My Side of the Mountain" Day could easily be adapted for any age group that reads the novel or has it read to them. The activities can be adapted for students in third through eighth grade, and can include all academic disciplines, as science gets interwoven with language arts, math, and social studies. And there are certainly plenty of physical education activities, as students hike up, down, and across the mountain. This program is scheduled to run the full school day with students returning home in time for their regular pickup.

Choosing a Site

If you are lucky, your school is located near the mountains where there are hundreds of thousands of acres of public and private lands available less than an hour's drive from school. However, not everyone is so fortunate.

An ideal site is one that is wooded, has a creek or two, and is semi-remote. While thousands of acres aren't necessary, the experience becomes more realistic when students get the feeling that they are in the wilderness. It really doesn't take a lot of land to get the feeling of being "one with nature."

It is definitely possible to do this program in a city park, on land owned by one of your students' families, or even on the school property if there is a wooded area away from normal school activity. A forested area does add much to the realism, but any site could be used with some modification to a few of the activities.

Sites that have a simple cabin adjoining or on the property itself are handy, as you can use the cabin as headquarters for the day and as a temporary shelter from the cold. After all, Sam was able to build a shelter inside a hemlock tree. If you can, keep a kettle of water on the fireplace to use for hot chocolate. You may even be lucky enough to find a local authority on the history of the area and have that guest stationed in the cabin to provide stories and insights into life in the mountains throughout the day.

Don't be surprised if your site has no indoor plumbing. This simple lack of modern necessities adds to the realism and harshness of the experience. Just prepare students (and parents) beforehand to the fact that they will need to do what Sam did when "nature calls." Be sure, however, to provide instruction in wilderness ethics for students and parents so they can indeed "find relief," if needed.

As with any activity on or off campus, there is always some risk of injury. Keep at least one vehicle with you at the site, have a well-stocked first-aid kit and the knowledge to use it, and know where phones are available. With today's electronic marvels, you may find a cellular phone gets a signal from your location. Leave a map to your site with your school in case there is an emergency and someone needs to find you. Common sense and preparation will help insure that your day is a safe experience. (Basic safety rules are included later in this chapter.)

Choosing the Day

There can be no right or wrong day for this experience since this program will remain in your students' memories for years to come. You might have students read *My Side of the Mountain* starting in mid-fall so you're finished with it around the end of November. A day in the winter (or colder months of the year) is a good choice since one of Sam's greatest obstacles is to make it through the winter. He describes in great detail what it feels like to be really cold, and providing this experience in the late fall or early winter does indeed get students to understand the situations Sam faces.

Enlisting Parent Volunteers

Teachers serve as "ring masters" and trouble-shooters, however, invite parents to serve as leaders. The more parents you can enlist, the smaller the student groups. Group size of four to five students per leader is ideal. With this ratio, everyone gets to have a truly hands-on experience.

Make sure parents receive the information and activity list beforehand. If possible, meet with parents before the trip. The activity sheets (pages 111–113) are simple enough. Ask parents to let students decide how to do an activity; parents are there for safety and supervision. Tell parents when to return to the gathering spot for the trip back to school, and give individual groups times of when to meet to make their fires with flint and steel.

Meeting with Students on the Day

Before setting everyone free, emphasize a few last-minute reminders.

- Students must stay with their groups throughout the day.

- This is not a race! Encourage students to work carefully to see that every step is completed to the best of their ability. You should not move to a new activity until you've done your best with the current one.

- Groups can organize their activities in any order they wish with the exception of fire building. A time for this activity will be assigned to each group.

- Groups will decide when and where to eat lunch.

- Remind students that they are guests in the wilderness and must return everything as they found it. They may not disturb any living thing—plant or animal. Any branches or limbs used must be found on the ground. Leave animal homes undisturbed. For example, if you move a log to look under it, you must carefully return the log to its original location.

- Students may not have a knife of any size. The leader may have one, but he or she alone will do any cutting. Challenge students to find whatever they need in the right size, or find a "wilderness way" of cutting something if cutting is an absolute must.

"My Side of the Mountain" Day Activities

The following activities have been chosen based on a mountain site. Most of them can be done just about anywhere. However, you will have to make final adjustments to suit your particular location. Once you have chosen your activities, make a student activity sheet that students can use to complete each activity. Based on the activities you choose, be sure to send home a list of items each student needs for this special day.

1. **Map the old Gribley homesite.** (This is the area you will be calling "headquarters.") Design symbols for various features. Use a compass to get the directions correctly noted on your maps. Make accurate measurements of various features such as location of the possible cabin site; possible crop areas; sources of drinking water; creeks; and nearby natural features such as large trees, ravines, large rocks, and so on. Make your map as accurate as possible so that another group could locate the features you've noted.

2. **Locate the best water source for the Gribley homesite.** Measure its distance to the homesite. Make sure to include this on the map. Can your group devise a way to get water from the source to the cabin site?

3. **Identify four different trees.** Estimate the height of each tree. Measure the circumference. Use a math formula to determine the diameter. Sketch these trees with names and measurements in your field journal.

4. **Locate the largest hemlock tree you can find.** (Remember, Sam's home was in a hemlock tree.) Measure the circumference of this tree. Locate this tree's location on your site map. Determine if this tree would be large enough in which to build a home.

5. **Build one simple camp tool or piece of rustic wilderness furniture.** Make sure all materials you use are found on the ground (use only natural materials). Sketch your creation in your field journal. Remember to disassemble your creation before leaving the area.

6. **Measure and record the water temperature of the creek in at least two places.** Do this at least twice during the day. Careful—don't slip!

7. **Build a simple animal trap and sketch it in your journal.** "Trip" your trap with a stick to see if it works. Note what type of animal it is designed to catch. Where would you place the trap to be most successful? Remember to completely dismantle this trap and return all of its components to the locations where you found them. No one should be able to find where you built this trap when you're done, especially unsuspecting animals.

8. **Measure and record the air temperature in at least three different locations.** Do this at least three times during the day—once within an hour of arriving, once at lunch, and the last time in the afternoon before departing.

9. **Find five signs of wildlife and sketch these in your journal.** Be on the alert. Wildlife may be in the basement, ground floor, or canopy of any tree. They may be under something as well. But remember, it is absolutely critical that you not disturb anything and that everything gets placed back exactly as you found it! Note in your journal what you think lives in the homes you've found.

10. **Start a fire using only flint and steel.** An inexpensive item from the Boy Scouts of America retailers called a "Hot Spark" can be used for this purpose. This item does a wonderful job of creating sizable sparks. You should have someone knowledgeable about fire safety help supervise this activity. When students successfully build a fire, you might let them take a minute and roast a few marshmallows to celebrate their success.

11. **After completing at least five activities, take ten minutes to reflect on what you have done so far and recap this in your journal.**

12. **Look for crayfish homes along the creek.** Try not to step in the water.

13. **Look for signs of other life around the creek, such as animal tracks or homes.** Sketch what you find in your journal.

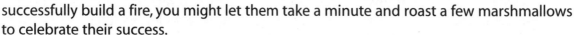
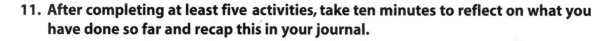

14. **Measure the velocity of the creek.** You can do this by dropping a small twig in the creek at one spot and see how long it takes to reach another point. Record these findings in your journal.

15. **Look for possible cabin sites for Sam and/or his family.** Why do you feel you've found the perfect site? Note your findings in your journal.

16. **Build a simple shelter, big enough for one person, out of materials you find on the ground.** Sketch this shelter in your journal. Try it out for size. If you're brave, pour some water on top to see if it will withstand the forces of nature. When finished, the shelter must be carefully dismantled and all parts returned to nature.

17. **Locate a ravine and place its location on your map.**

18. **Give the creek and other places you discover a name.** Add these to your notes.

19. **Sit very quietly for 10–15 minutes and look and listen for signs of wildlife.** First, find a spot for your group to be alone. Then sit quietly and list what you hear and see in your journal. You may even want to try to camouflage yourselves.

20. **Look for edible plants.** DO NOT eat them.

Follow-up Activities for Back at School

Once "My Side of the Mountain" Day is over, you can use the experience for additional learning opportunities back in the classroom. Below are some suggested activities to get you started. These activities can serve as an excellent closure and assessment to your day-long program.

1. **Write a story about what you feel happened to the family that once lived at the site where we had our experience.**

2. **Write a summary of your day spent "on the mountain."**

3. **Write a journal entry describing the "cold" or being out in the elements on a winter day.** Make sure to include how you feel you would handle the first night out by yourself.

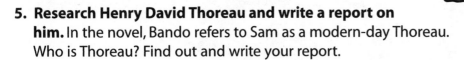

4. **Write a journal entry about whether you would like to live like Sam for a year.** If a year is too long, what about a month or a week? Explain your feelings in your journal.

5. **Research Henry David Thoreau and write a report on him.** In the novel, Bando refers to Sam as a modern-day Thoreau. Who is Thoreau? Find out and write your report.

6. **Write a letter to your parents telling them you are planning on spending a year in the woods by yourself.** Give reasons why you feel you are ready for and able to handle this experience.

7. **Research the history of the land where we held our experience.**

8. **Build a model of the inside of a tree home like Sam's.**

114

9. **Make a list of the skills you think you would need to spend a year living like Sam.**
   Where do you think you could learn those skills?

10. **Read one "how-to" book on outdoor living.**

11. **Make a display of the work you did on "My Side of the Mountain" Day.**
    Use the notes you made in your field journal.

12. **Think of one or two other activities we should add to our activities list for next year.**

Final Thoughts

This program is a tremendous educational opportunity to bring learning outdoors. The added benefit of building team spirit by emphasizing cooperative learning is a definite plus. Kids and parents love this chance to be outdoors working together in this unique teaching environment. You will find the experience to be an outstanding way to build excellent public relations for your school. Invite your principal to join your class, possibly even as a group leader. The parents involved will come to understand how worthwhile special off-campus educational opportunities can be.

The excitement will continue as you allow student groups to share their discoveries and adventures of their special day during follow-up class discussions. The follow-up activities help insure that the learning that took place on this day extends for weeks. Start making plans now for your own version of "My Side of the Mountain" Day. It is sure to be one of the highlights of your school year!

Good Stories

Stories are excellent ways of closing a campfire and ending an outdoor education program. Nothing captures the attention of children more easily than a good story. It's easy to find stories with a message that are worth retelling. The following are two favorite stories to get you started. Each has a moral that helps children learn some of life's valuable lessons. They have been shortened considerably, so embellish them any way you like.

Two Brothers

(Moral: You get what you expect.)

Two boys were going to a new school one day. Both were a little nervous about making new friends, meeting their teachers, and learning new routines. Their parents got lost on the way to school and stopped at a house where an old man was out watering his garden. It so happened that this old man was the neighborhood "wise man."

The old "wise man" saw that the family needed help, and he asked them if he could be of service. After asking directions, the first boy asked the man what the kids were like at that school. The old man thought for a few moments and said, "Well son, what are the children like where you came from?" The boy replied that they were all jerks and show-offs, and he couldn't stand them. He continued to belittle his old school.

The wise old man then said, "Well, you're going to find your new school exactly like your old one. Good luck."

The boy uttered, "I knew it!" and stomped back to his parents' car. He was so upset that he forget the directions, so the father sent his other son back to ask the old man once more. The old man didn't mind giving directions again, as he knew the first boy was so incensed that he wouldn't remember them anyway.

As the second boy was turning to leave, he thought he would ask about his new school, too. "What are the kids like at the school?" he queried.

The old man didn't have to think too long before he asked his same question, "What are the kids like where you used to go to school?" The boy replied that they were great kids, he loved his school, and he hoped his new one would be just as nice.

The wise old man said, "Well son, you're going to find your new school exactly like your old one."

The Strawberries

(Moral: Make the most of your life today.)

A man (woman, student, or whoever you choose) was hiking one day when he heard footsteps behind him. He didn't think too much of it, but the footsteps seemed to be following him. He started to walk a little faster, and the footsteps matched his cadence, step for step. It was time for a quick over-the-shoulder glance. Behind him was a bear—a big one—and the bear seemed hungry. In fact, the man figured *he* was probably the intended dinner.

The man started running, and so did the bear. The man ran until his strength was gone. Just when he thought he couldn't make it any farther, he saw a rock wall ahead of him. It appeared that the wall was separated from the trail by a deep chasm. And with just seconds left, he saw some roots that were breaking out of the wall. If he could just make it to the edge, he knew his only chance was to jump and hope he could grab on to one of those roots. Then he could only pray that the roots would hold his weight just long enough for him to catch his breath. And then maybe, just maybe, he could pull himself up to the top of the wall and reach safety.

With his last remaining breath, he took that giant leap of faith. Miraculously, he was able to grasp a root, and though it strained under his weight, it held. His heart was pounding; he was so relieved. The bear stayed right there reaching out with its massive clawed paws, but the man was just scarcely out of its reach.

After the man rested a bit, he felt he had recovered enough of his strength and composure to try and scramble to the top. He inched his way up until he could peer over the wall. The man sighed with relief.

Then, out of nowhere, a second bear appeared! This one was larger and meaner than the first. It took a giant lunge at the man, who quickly backed down to his safe area. The second bear kept growling and reaching its paw down toward him. He didn't know what to do!

While he was waiting and contemplating his life, the man looked next to him. Right within reach, he eyed the most luscious-looking red strawberries he had ever seen. He thought for a moment and then reached over and took one. He smelled it, turned it over in his hands, then popped it into his mouth and ate it. It was delicious! The man grabbed another and another and ate them all. And that's the end of the story.

(Students will be wildly miffed that the story ends here. They want to know what happened to the man. Did the man feed the bears? Explain the moral of the story: You can't always worry about the past, and you can't always worry about the future. So while you're here in this time and place, make the most of it. Make the most of life. Make the most of today.)

Chapter Seven

Building and Equipping Your Own Outdoor Center

Imagine having the best field trips right at your school! That can happen using the ideas found in this chapter.

Now that you are a pro at taking your students outdoors, it's time to share what you've learned with others. An outdoor center could become a focal point of your school. This chapter contains over a dozen great ideas to include in your center. You could even combine these with some of the discovery center ideas on pages 34 and 35. You'll make your school the envy of every school in the city! You might even motivate the local nature center to come and get ideas from you!

Your Outdoor Center

O n pages 34 and 35 you read about starting a classroom nature corner or school discovery center. This chapter will help you design and build a curriculum-integrated, wide-reaching outdoor center for a reasonably small amount of money. Once you make this proposal, civic clubs, the PTA, and even your principal will usually help you with funding. An outdoor center will offer students the opportunity to participate in the many activities described in this book.

You Need Space

First, you're going to need some space. It doesn't have to be huge, but it should be on or adjacent to school grounds. Places away from school can become a problem. There are too many obstacles involved for impromptu or even planned trips off school property. If you can't find space at or adjacent to your school, try adding what you can to your nature corner or school discovery center and leave it at that. Note: This plan has been designed for under $500, providing the space that is available to you is free.

What Kind of Space Do You Need?

The ideal space would include trees, open areas (some with grass), and a pristine gurgling creek. Chances are, you're not going to get all of this. However, regardless of the area you end up with, you will still be able to do many of the study stations listed below and on pages 34 and 35. Many of these study stations can achieve the same results in a variety of locations.

Group Dynamics Area—This is space set aside for all those group dynamics activities you read about on pages 82–94. Since you're going to have the space and a little money, you could also build a few simple props to help with your instruction.

Outdoor Classroom—This is a simple meeting area with rustic seating. Use this for teaching any subject, not just those related to the outdoors.

Treehouse Observation Station—A simple structure built several feet into the air for observing and appreciating nature from a new perspective is a great place for teaching and learning. Be sure the structure has sturdy railings and safe access. (Don't let students build this. Perhaps the local high school vocational carpentry class could come to your rescue.)

Various Nature Trails—Include trails that emphasize interpretation, tuning in the senses, and environmental concepts. You could even include a writing trail. Each year, your new class could help brainstorm, design, and build a new addition.

Orienteering Course—Include an area for teaching basic map and compass skills. The very least you could do is post *North, South, East,* and *West* markers and use the area for simple mapping practice and measuring skills.

Archaeological Dig Area—Even if there is nothing to dig for, this could be a great learning experience. Students will learn to pay careful attention to every detail when sifting through shovels of dirt. You could always seed an area with things to look for. (See page 23 for more information on running your own Dinosaur Dig.)

Gardening Area—This is another good place for students to get dirty while enjoying science firsthand. If the climate in your locale is cooperative, you will hopefully get to enjoy the fruits of your labor during the school year.

Composting Area—Another good place to teach ecological concepts is in a composting area. This can also be used for getting rid of some of that lunchroom waste.

Weather Station—You can make this as elaborate or as simple as your funds allow. If all else fails, you can always install a trusty 100% accurate "weather rock." To do this, hang a rock from a string and include a sign nearby with notes about weather forecasting, such as *If rock is wet, it's raining; If rock is dry, it's clear; If rock is moving, it's windy; If rock is white, it's snowing; If rock is hot, it's sunny;* and so on. As old as this joke is, kids and parents still get a kick out of it.

120

Wildlife Feeding Station—Research what types of plants and ground cover you need to attract native wildlife to your center. You might even consider building a nearby blind to keep excited youngsters hidden. You can probably get started by using this spot to stack all the brush you've already cleared getting this far with your outdoor center.

Curriculum Paths—Perhaps each department at your school could design a short path with stations emphasizing skills and concepts in its area of study. The possibilities are endless. You could have a writing trail for language arts, fitness stations for physical education, artist benches for drawing activities, an area for measuring and estimating for math, a fallen log with the rings marked by years for a social studies time line, and so on. And of course, the entire area provides unlimited uses for science.

Plant Succession Area—Plant succession is more easily taught if it can be observed. Rope or fence off a small area of cleared space to use as a study station. Students will be able to see for themselves how cleared areas start to regenerate over time. You may want to post a sign giving the date of the original clearing, and one reminding the grounds crew not to cut in this area.

Recycling Area—Perhaps this should stay in the school or by the maintenance area. You could, however, include a spot at your outdoor center where students can leave things that need to be recycled, such as trail guides (to be used again), paper that needs to be sent in for recycling, and aluminum cans.

Camp Site—Clear an area that could be used for bringing small groups in to spend the night. Include a few picnic tables and a safe spot for a small campfire. This might be more than you care to offer, but you can be sure your students will enjoy camping out with their classmates and teachers—even if you don't. You'll need help (lots of it) and access to the bathrooms and school for small emergencies requiring a phone, and for weathering any unexpected storms. You'll finally be able to talk about the planets and constellations in nature's own planetarium.

Resources

This chapter contains an abundance of information to keep you going strong. The organizations listed provide books, materials, and even training in a variety of outdoor education areas. Three of the organizations—Institute for Earth Education, National Science Teachers Association, and the National Wildlife Federation— offer memberships with various member benefits.

While this book may be the only such resource you'll need to run programs for years, the titles listed under *Books and Other Sources* will give you even more possibilities. You'll also find catalogs to write away for. There are several companies and associations who publish helpful catalogs of additional books about all areas of outdoor education, as well as sell needed equipment for naturalists, such as bug boxes, plant presses, and hand lenses. You'll be able to equip your own discovery center from the mailbox!

Organizations

Institute for Earth Education

Cedar Cove
Greenville, WV 24945
(304) 832-6404

The Institute for Earth Education publishes entire packaged programs for teaching others to love the earth. Write for their *Earth Education Sourcebook*, which offers program materials, inspirational books, and hard-to-find props. IEE also offers workshops at sites around the world.

National Science Teachers Association

1840 Wilson Blvd.
Arlington, VA 22201
(703) 243-7100

The NSTA has been helping teachers teach science for years. Membership comes with your choice of journals geared to specific grade levels. NSTA sponsors several excellent conventions held around the United States each year.

Project Adventure, Inc.

P.O. Box 100
Hamilton, MA 01936
(978) 468-7981

Project Adventure has been a leader in adventure education for 25 years. They sell books, ropes-course supplies and materials, group-initiatives props, and so on, and offer workshops at sites around the United States on all aspects of group initiatives programming.

National Wildlife Federation

Attn: Education Dept.
8925 Leesburg Pike
Vienna, VA 22184
(703) 790-4100

The National Wildlife Federation is synonymous with protecting our planet. In addition to their line of magazines, NWF offers several resources for educators, including *Animal Tracks*, a classroom resource. NWF also offers extended outdoor learning adventures for adults called "Conservation Summits," and helps families and schools interested in starting backyard wildlife habitats.

National Project Wild
707 Conservation Lane, Suite 305
Gaithersburg, MD 20878
(301) 527-8900

National Project Wild coordinates the Project Wild and Aquatic Wild programs throughout the United States. Each state offers teacher workshops several times throughout the year. Participants in these workships receive plenty of excellent reference materials, including the well-known *Project Wild* and *Aquatic Wild* activity books.

American Forest Foundation
Attn: Project Learning Tree
1111 19th Street, NW, Suite 780
Washington, DC 20036
(202) 463-2462

Project Learning Tree (PLT) offers workshops for educators throughout the United States using the nation's forest as their primary focus. Participants receive an activity guide brimming with things to try. Each state has an office that coordinates these workshops.

Books and Other Sources

Bag of Tricks and *Bag of Tricks II*
by Jane Sanborn
Search Publications
P.O. Box 167
Florissant, CO 80816

These books contain a myriad of group dynamics and nature activities from a long-time camp person.

Cowstails and Cobras II, Silver Bullets, The Bottomless Bag Again, The Bottomless Bag Live, and *Quicksilver*
by Karl Rohnke
Kendall/Hunt Publishing Company
P.O. Box 1840
Dubuque, IA 52004

These are all books by Karl Rohnke, one of the masters of group dynamics and founder of Project Adventure.

124

50 Simple Things Kids Can Do to Save the Earth
by John Javna
Andrews and McMeel
4900 Main Street
Kansas City, MO 64112

This book contains ideas to get kids started in the conservation movement.

**Humanizing Environmental Education: A Guide for Leading Nature
and Human Nature Activities**
by Clifford E. Knapp and Joel Goodman
American Camping Association
5000 State Road 67 North
Martinsville, IN 46151

This book contains tons of ideas to help you run your whole outdoor education program, including some scheduling ideas for a long-term experience.

Making the Most of Today: Daily Readings for Young People on Self-Awareness, Creativity, and Self-Esteem
by Pamela Espeland and Rosemary Wallner
Free Spirit Publishing, Inc.
400 First Avenue North, Suite 616
Minneapolis, MN 55401

This resource includes positive messages for each day of the year. This is a wonderful resource to use as discussion starters for team-building programs.

Sharing Nature with Children and **Sharing the Joy of Nature**
by Joseph Cornell
Dawn Publications
14618 Tyler Foote Road
Nevada City, CA 95959

These classic books contain dozens of environmental awareness activities.

Sunship Earth and **Acclimatization**
by Steve Van Matre
American Camping Association
5000 State Road 67 North
Martinsville, IN 46151

These books show you new ways of teaching environmental concepts. The Sunship Earth program is offered at outdoor education centers around the world.

The World Wide Web

The World Wide Web is an excellent source for finding information. Use key words *outdoor education* and *environmental education* to start your searches. Many of the organizations mentioned have home pages on the Web, and those that do will provide current information on local contacts. Some of the Web sites even have activities for you to try.

Places to Write for Catalogs

American Camping Association
5000 State Road 67 North
Martinsville, IN 46151-7902
(765) 342-8456

The ACA catalog sells books on all types of outdoor subjects, including environmental education, team building, and nature crafts.

Delta Education
12 Simon Street
P.O. Box 3000
Nashua, NH 03061
(800) 442-5444

Delta sells plenty of kid-sized science equipment and books perfect for your outdoor center or classroom nature corner. They are also the publishers of the *Outdoor Biology Instructional Strategies* (OBIS) materials that are wonderful for teaching environmental concepts and other nature-oriented phenomena.

Learned Enterprises International
W9115 Bluewaters Pass
Cambridge, WI 53523
(800) 462-0411

LEI publishes books, games, and offers workshops and other resources for teaching trust and team building.

Museum Products

84 Route 27
Mystic, CT 06355
(800) 395-5400

The Museum Products catalog is filled with supplies you'll soon find you can't live without, especially if you're operating your own nature museum or discovery center.

National Science Teachers Association

1840 Wilson Blvd.
Arlington, VA 22201-3000
(703) 243-7100

NSTA publishes a catalog filled with hundreds of books on teaching and appreciating science, nature, and the environment for teachers of all grade levels.

Acknowledgments

Most of the activities acknowledged below can be found in the references in some form or another. Many of you will know these games from your own childhood, though you may have called them by a different name. Acknowledged here are the published sources from where I first learned of a particular activity. Thanks to all the authors and/or publishers for their willingness to share.

Envirolopes, Food-Chain Game, and *Adaptation-Predator-Prey* are from OBIS with permission. Delta Education, Inc. All rights reserved. Permission granted to classroom teachers to photocopy for classroom use only. Not for resale, redistribution, or use other than the classroom without further permission. Delta Education, Inc., P.O. Box 915, Hudson, NH 03051.

Hug Tag, Triangle Tag, Impulse, Data Processing, Last Detail, Knots, and *Lap Sit* are from the books *The New Games Book* and *More New Games* by Andrew Fluegelman. 1976 & 1981. Used with permission of Doubleday Publishing Company, New York, NY.

Stranded comes from *Cowstails and Cobras* by Karl Rohnke. 1977. Used with permission of the author. Kendall/Hunt Publishing Company, Dubuque, IA.

Team Sense and some of the scavenger hunt themes are from *Bag of Tricks* by Jane Sanborn. 1984. Used with permission of the author. Search Publications, Florissant, CO.

Some of the *Sharing Circle* topics are from *Humanizing Environmental Education* by Clifford Knapp and Joel Goodman. 1981. Reprinted by permission of the publisher, American Camping Association, Martinsville, IN.

Meet a Tree, Noah's Ark, Sleeping Miser, and *Bats and Moths* are from *Sharing Nature with Children* by Joseph Cornell. 1979. Used with permission of the publisher, Dawn Publications, Nevada City, CA.

Magic Spots and *Waste Watchers* are from *Sunship Earth* by Steve Van Matre. 1979. Reprinted with permission of the publisher, American Camping Association, Martinsville, IN.

With lots of appreciation I would also like to thank:

- Bobbie Levin, my wife and best friend, for her wonderful ideas, understanding, and patience when I'm gone on yet another trip.
- Frank Bell, Sr. (Chief), the first person who taught me that a true university could be a log with a mentor at one end and a child at the other.
- Steve Van Matre, a genius when it comes to creating true magic in the outdoors.
- Roland Doepner, an education professor who convinced me that teaching was neat.
- Kim Broshar, my co-teacher, who bestows her wonderful outdoor education knowledge and ideas on me and our fifth graders on a daily basis.
- Claudia Sherry, my boss, for letting me try just about anything once.